MW00583515

Johnny Sophomore

Johnny Manziel's
Final Year
at Texas A&M

Derek Worlow

For Ainsley
Because you save me with your laughter and stories

For Chloe
Because you save me with your strength and heart

For Granddad
Because you passed to me a love of the written word

With love I dedicate this book to the three of you

Table of Contents

"This is a moment that I've dreamed about since I've been a kid – running around the backyard pretending I was Doug Flutie, throwing a Hail Mary to my dad. Now I'm so blessed to be on the stage with such a group of great guys and to be invited into this fraternity – what a pleasure it really is...It's such an honor to represent Texas A&M and my teammates here tonight, I wish they could be on the stage with me. Texas A&M, choosing that school is one of the best decisions I've ever made in my entire life and I'm so proud to be a part of that. To Mom, Dad, Meri and the entire family watching – you mean the world to me. I just want to thank you for the encouragement, the love and the patience over the years...Most of all I want to thank God for allowing me to be here. All that He's blessed me with in my entire life I'm thankful for. For the love and the grace You have shown me, I'll be forever grateful. The values that I have learned from my parents and that have carried over by Texas A&M – leadership, respect and putting others first is what the 12th Man is all about. I believe the 12th Man is one of the greatest traditions in all of college football – 40,000 students standing not as fans but as members of our team. To the 12th Man, Texas A&M, Kerrville, Texas and Aggies everywhere – this Heisman Trophy is for you."

Johnny Manziel
Heisman Acceptance Speech
New York, New York
December 8, 2012

1 Spring Game

As Johnny Manziel walked onto the immaculate grass of Kyle Field, he understood how much he needed this. It had been months since he played in the Cotton Bowl and life had turned bizarre in the space between. In a brilliant early April sunshine, Manziel began to warm up as fans entered the stadium. As his right arm loosened, he broke away from the demands of his surreal existence. He laughed with teammates, sang along with the pregame music, and felt better than he had in a long while.

Once the Maroon and White spring game started, Manziel showed the 45,000 in attendance that despite what they read or heard or feared, football remained the most necessary thing in his life. His passes were crisp and accurate, on rollouts he hit his receivers in stride, and in the pocket he looked patient and mature. With every completion, the crowd cheered with delight. He was the reason they had turned out in record numbers. Maybe on a national level Manziel was becoming a pariah, but to the hardcore Texas A&M fan he continued to be a god worthy of virginal sacrifice.

The problem for Manziel was he could not please them all. Some wanted, even demanded, that the quarterback maintain a ritual of reckless Saturdays leading the Aggies, then downshift into elderly helping choirboy once the game was over. He wasn't built this way nor did he have any inclination to adhere to these unrealistic standards. To Manziel, one had to understand his personality was not something he could simply stop, as if there was a knob he could turn and shut down what made him the best quarterback in college football. He was going to live this life as he saw fit. This did not prevent the criticism from stinging Manziel. He begged for his detractors to see things from his perspective. Instead of identifying with the Heisman Trophy winner, Manziel was slapped with the label of spoiled ingrate.

After the Heisman everybody wanted a piece of Johnny Football. He dreaded going to his parents' home because all he did was sign his name over and over and over. He hired bodyguards to watch over him and became solemn because of all the attention on gossip websites like TMZ. Rumors began to spread that Manziel had become attracted to the nightlife as a way to cope with the pain of losing his anonymity.

Opinions sprouted claiming Manziel was his own worst enemy. The kid could not keep his life, or his mouth, off of Twitter and Instagram, and all the anguish he endured was undoubtedly self-inflicted, they believed. This particular point of view held considerable merit but certainly lacked empathy. Regardless of the righteous venom, Manziel was still a young man whose life flipped in just over four months. In September of 2012 he was starting his first collegiate football game. By December, he had won the sports world's most prestigious trophy. In the weeks that followed, Manziel's life became both playground and prison.

This internal conflict took center stage in one of Manziel's final plays that spring game day. With the A&M quarterback crouched several yards behind center, Manziel took the shotgun snap and gave the ball to Brandon Williams. In theory, his job was done. Manziel should have stepped back, and watched Williams finish the run. He did not do this. He ran as quickly as he could, pulling ahead of the running back. Manziel looked for someone to block, or more accurately, someone to hit. It would be four months until he was back on this field where everything made sense. Now, in this uncatchable moment, Manziel was having a hard time letting go.

During his junior year at Kerrville Tivy High School, Johnny Manziel accounted for 2,782 yards through the air, 1,529 yards on the ground, and crossed the goal line an astonishing 52 times.

His reward for the phenomenal year was something more absurd than the numbers he accumulated. Not one major collegiate football program in the state of Texas offered Manziel a scholarship to play quarterback.

Manziel had to travel to California, the summer before his final high school season, to be discovered. It was there at a throwing camp that Manziel caught the eye of Oregon head coach Chip Kelly. Kelly, known for his innovative, up-tempo offense, was taken with Manziel's mobility, his accurate arm and his instinct to create under pressure. Kelly believed he had discovered a hidden Texas superstar much like Baylor head coach Art Briles had found with Robert Griffin III. The Ducks head coach convinced the Manziel family not to return to Texas after the camp concluded but rather to travel to Eugene, Oregon and visit the Oregon campus. The Manziel's, frustrated by the lack of attention from schools like Texas, TCU and Texas Tech, jumped at the chance to tour the tremendous Nike financed facilities of the University of Oregon.

Johnny was responsive to the red carpet treatment Kelly bestowed upon him. When Oregon extended a scholarship to Manziel, the Kerrville Tivy product did not hesitate in orally accepting the offer. The agreement was not binding until Manziel could sign a Letter of Intent in February of the upcoming year. Johnny remained eligible to visit other schools and more importantly to Oregon, he could switch his commitment from the Ducks.

As we know, Manziel never made it to the Pacific Northwest. The man responsible for this change in the quarterback's plan was Tom Rossley. A veteran coach of 32 years with time in both the professional and amateur ranks, Rossley was the

quarterbacks coach for then Texas A&M head coach
Mike Sherman.

Sherman's A&M staff was late to the party
recruiting Manziel. After viewing his junior year
highlight film, Sherman dispatched Rossley to watch
the quarterback throw. In Manziel, Rossley shared the
opinion of Kelly in believing the soon-to-be senior had
the makeup of an elite quarterback. Rossley was not
deterred by the measurements of Manziel that forced
other programs to dismiss the young signal caller.
Instead of dwelling on the size of Manziel (arguably
six feet, one inch, and 190 pounds), Rossley saw a
clone of one of his former players, Super Bowl
champion Brett Favre. Manziel shared the vision, the
tenacity, and the heart of Favre in Rossley's eyes. "I
was enamored with (Manziel). He's a difference
maker and a special guy," said Rossley. The now
retired coach loved the quarterback's determination to
never surrender a down. "He wants to win every
play," Rossley said.

Although Rossley loved Manziel he was not
the one who made the ultimate decision on
scholarships. Sherman's hesitation in showing nothing
more than a passing interest in the quarterback led
Manziel to choose Oregon. However, after word of
Manziel's commitment to Oregon reached Rossley, the
quarterbacks coach convinced Sherman that Johnny
was still a possibility for A&M, but they would need to
be aggressive. Sherman responded by immediately
making Manziel a scholarship offer to play quarterback
for the Aggies. Rossley felt Manziel wanted to stay

close to home and play football but the commitment to Oregon would be extremely difficult to get him to turn away from. "It was hard for him because he's such a high integrity guy," Rossley said.

Fall weekends during that senior season were busy for the Manziel family. On Friday nights in Kerrville, Johnny constructed a final season that made heads turn across the nation. 5300 yards of total offense and 77 touchdowns led to Manziel being named to Parade's All American team. Then on Saturdays, the family traveled to College Station where Rossley sold Johnny on the virtues of an education (and football career) at Texas A&M. "I kept telling (Manziel's parents), 'He's a legend in Texas. You don't want to let him leave Texas and be a legend somewhere else,'" Rossley said.

The plan worked. As Manziel became a staple at A&M home games, Rossley made a point to greet the family before his coaching duties called. "When he kept coming, I knew we had a chance to flip him. One of the last games he came to, he had an Aggie T-shirt on and I thought, 'Now we're talking,'" Rossley said. Manziel switched his commitment to A&M. It was the first of several dominoes to fall giving Johnny Football the opportunity to make history.

Around the time Johnny Manziel first landed upon the campus of Texas A&M, the landscape of college football was awash in rumors of wholesale change. Gossip of schools jumping from conference to super conference flooded the airwaves and filled countless articles in newspapers. A&M entered this world of hearsay when speculation grew that the school would move, along with Texas, Oklahoma and Oklahoma State, to create a supersized Pacific 16 conference.

Texas A&M, unknown to Pac-12 officials, had other ideas for their future.

In late September of 2011, as rumors hit a feverish level, officials at the university decided enough was enough. Exhausted by years of being thrown around by the bratty whims of the University of Texas, A&M agreed to join in the Southeastern Conference as their first ever member from the state of Texas. The move was fueled, in large part, by the University of Texas agreeing with ESPN to create the Longhorn Network. The 24/7 all-Texas, all-the-time channel would pump roughly $20 million dollars into the Texas coffers each year. The boost in revenue made Texas the richest program in college football with a yearly haul exceeding $100 million. With tremendous power, Texas began welcoming suitors for a potential conference move. Schools such as Texas A&M were left to follow and be included, or risk leaving on their own. The prospect of the latter was undeniably fraught with the possibility of being denied tens of millions of dollars in television money, media exposure, and by extension, relevance.

A&M's flirtation with the SEC introduced the university to the reasons why the conference was the crown jewel of college football. Each week the

17

football games of the SEC reached 66 million homes. Powered by television deals with CBS and ESPN, the tremendously wealthy conference divided their money evenly amongst members. This placated any possible fears A&M officials may have had that the University of Alabama might run off and pull the same stunt Texas did with the Longhorn Network. Texas A&M agreed to move to the SEC.

At the press conference to announce the change, A&M President R. Bowen Loftin made the remark that the move was a "100 year decision." The university felt the conference would allow them to reach heights it had never attained before. "There is absolutely no hierarchy within the SEC," Loftin said. "Every member is equally valued, at the table for every decision that's made and treated with genuine respect." It didn't take much of a decoder ring to know who Loftin was referring to with his statement.

Word of the desertion came with the additional announcement that Texas A&M would begin to compete in the SEC in less than one year. There was little time to waste if change were to be made to the struggling football program under Sherman. So after another mediocre season in 2011, A&M officials decided to fire Sherman. The search for the man to lead A&M into a new era quickly zeroed in on University of Houston head coach Kevin Sumlin. The coach, who had ties to A&M with a stint as offensive assistant under former A&M head coach R.C. Slocum, had become one of the nation's hottest young head coaching candidates. Sumlin, coming off 35 wins in four seasons as the Cougars head coach, did not hesitate in agreeing to a contract that would pay him roughly $2 million per season. "Aggieland is a special place," Sumlin said in a statement. "I look forward to working with the young men in the football program and recruiting the type of players we need to be successful in the SEC." Sumlin, the first African American head coach to ever be hired by Texas A&M, would not have to look hard for talent to be successful. Sherman had been generous enough to leave the cupboard full of special athletes on his way out.

With Ryan Tannehill, a senior on his way to the NFL, entrenched as the Aggies' 2011 starting quarterback, Sherman decided that Manziel would best help Texas A&M by sitting his freshman year on the sidelines. The move to redshirt Manziel was designed to give the freshman a chance to grow physically as well as allow extra time for him to become familiar with Sherman's pro-style offense. The decision to fire Sherman, forced Manziel back to square one, needing to prove his worth all over again.

It is customary with any coaching change for there to be an information swap between the old regime and new staff. When Sumlin sat down with Tom Rossley, the former quarterbacks coach touted Manziel as the one to take A&M to the next level. An entire spring and summer evaluation led the new head coach to agree, and the announcement was made that Manziel would be the 2012 starter for Texas A&M.

Manziel's first game of the 2012 season was to be a road trip to play Louisiana Tech but Hurricane Isaac spoiled those plans. The postponement made the home game versus Florida, A&M's first ever SEC conference game, Manziel's college football debut. A difficult 20-17 loss to the Gators gave only a marginal glimpse to the run Manziel and the Aggies were about to embark upon. After the loss to the Gators, Texas A&M won 11 of their final 12 games. Manziel became a revelation with playmaking ability that rendered commentators speechless. He broke Archie Manning's 43-year SEC record for total offense in a single game, became the only player in SEC history to gain over 5000 yards in a single season, defeated top ranked Alabama on the road, humiliated Oklahoma in the Cotton Bowl, and became the first freshman to ever win the Heisman. It was a performance no one anticipated, and created a media firestorm that knew no saturation point. Johnny Manziel became Johnny Football, a persona embraced by the young quarterback both on and off the field. And everyone was waiting to see what the young man had planned for the encore.

Minutes before the A&M spring game began, offensive and defensive coaches went over, with their players, the rules and expectations for the glorified scrimmage. The offensive coaching staff encouraged execution. They wanted to see crisp passes, steady blocks, and no drops from the receivers. In the defensive huddle, the players were reminded to follow through on their assignments, maintain proper position via their footwork, and one last thing – no one, under any circumstance, was to hit Manziel.

In what surely garnered an ironic laugh or two, Manziel was outfitted in a black Adidas jersey for the spring game. The color was not meant to signal "villain" to those watching on ESPN but rather as a visual cue to defenders that Manziel was not to be contacted under any circumstance. This directive did not cover the reality Manziel created by pitching the ball to Williams and running full steam into the mass of colliding maroon and white jerseys.

The Aggie quarterback entered the fray and found a target – the walk-on safety Sam Moeller. Moeller had little time to avoid Manziel and luckily for him, he did not have to, as Manziel dove for Moeller's knees and badly missed.

Williams did not need the Manziel escort as he walked into the end zone untouched. The crowd boomed in approval as the referee raised his arms to signal touchdown. The A&M coaches boomed too as several rushed Manziel, and in many unprintable words, condemned the chop block effort the quarterback attempted. Johnny was told never to put a teammate or himself at risk like that again. An emasculated Manziel found Moeller and apologized.

The play was indicative of the struggle Manziel was facing on the verge of his sophomore season. There were more questions, more doubt filling the quarterback's mind than answers or hope. All around him people were whispering "National

Championship" and Manziel certainly wanted nothing more than to share something as special as a BCS title with his teammates. But the intensity of expectation left Manziel feeling more and more paranoid and cautious about being used. He was having a hard time balancing the control he enjoyed while playing and the helplessness he experienced once the game was over.

Looking ahead, Manziel believed the independence offered by the NFL would alleviate many of his burdens, but to be drafted where he wanted, he would need a season markedly better than his Heisman run of 2012. This was a daunting prospect to fathom for a quarterback that just made history. Manziel would have to fight in ways he never imagined, ignoring an intense media focus that rivaled the attention lavished upon high profile celebrity divorces. He would need to navigate a new way of living where he had no previous understanding, no steady guidance, and each day would offer Manziel a fresh chance to be humiliated on a grand stage.

There is always an opportunity in America for the ridiculed celebrity to appeal for empathy. Manziel's chance to publicly right his perceived wrongs was on the horizon. But first he had a life to enjoy and those days for Manziel would not be silent. He would head into the 2013 season screaming, thrashing, and furiously embracing the benefits the Heisman granted. Many believed the A&M quarterback deserved punishment for the ride he enjoyed over the months following his life altering award. They were hungry for Manziel's fall from grace and cheered loudly when the quarterback was beset by scandals created by his own hand.

2 Media Day

Johnny Manziel entered the Wynfrey Hotel, in Hoover, Alabama, a sharp dressed man. Walking through the lobby in a tailored blue suit, with complementary checkered shirt and diagonal striped tie, Manziel was flanked by several sleep deprived public relations professionals. They were there to see the execution of their plan to rehabilitate the image of Johnny Football. It was a script Manziel continued to rewrite in the hours leading up to his mea culpa. If Manziel was feeling guilt for the strain his public relations team displayed, he did not show it. By looking at him, one might believe he was the most relaxed man ever to soon be placed in front of a firing squad.

What forced Manziel to the Wynfrey in the middle of July, was the obligation known as SEC Media Days. The annual event, recently expanded in duration to accommodate the growth and spreading popularity of the conference, would play host to over 1,200 media members. Commentators, columnists, and bloggers from the arena of television, radio and the internet would all get their chance to pummel the brightest young football players the SEC had to offer with the most inane questions they could conjure.

To borrow from Will Ferrell's creation Ron Burgundy, the media event had become "a big deal." Most of the marquee press conferences were now broadcast live via all spectrums of delivery. Proving the event's significance, or rather because they had just agreed to flood the conference and its' members with hundreds of millions of dollars in a deal to create the SEC Network, ESPN was given permission to commandeer the hotel's lobby. With their large set perched on a heavily lighted stage, the network was the first stop for one-on-one interviews with legendary coaches Nick Saban and Les Miles and NFL grade players such as Jadeveon Clowney and A.J. McCarron. Manziel would be next.

By passing various credentialed members of the press, word began to spread that Manziel was in the building. His small entourage swiftly grew to a following herd. As he climbed onto the ESPN stage and sat to be fitted with a microphone, tens of journalists hungry to hear Manziel speak had surrounded the dais. The most desired interview subject at SEC Media Days adjusted his jacket and moved to the front of the chair as the set producer counted down the seconds. The well-coached, upright Heisman winner looked as calm as a Hindu cow when ESPN host Joe Tessitore cut a wicked grin and asked Manziel, "Anything going on this morning?" The quarterback's smile widened. "Not a thing," Manziel said. "Just another day."

It would be anything other than an ordinary day for Manziel. For many in the crowd, many watching in College Station, and those closest to the quarterback, the young man had much to explain. He could start by clarifying what took place in a late-night incident that occurred over a year ago.

Johnny Manziel's first and only arrest came in the early hours of June 29th, 2012. Within a section of College Station known as Northgate, a patrolling police officer came upon two males engaged in what the officer would later describe as a "mutual combat." The area is a common ground for police to pass through as it is populated by a strip of bars that run parallel to the Texas A&M campus. The patrolman, aided by arriving backup, broke up the fight and separated the sparring men – an African American male in his late forties and a Caucasian male believed to be in his late teens. Once apart, statements were taken. The time was 2 A.M.

The teenager, later identified as Manziel, was asked to provide proper identification. The questioning officer was handed a Louisiana State driver's license showing Manziel's age to be 21. Skeptical of the authenticity of the identifications the officer asked Manziel for his birthdate.

This is where the ruse fell apart.

Manziel correctly answered the month and day of his birthdate but wavered on the birth year. First he said it was 1992, when asked again later in the interview, Manziel claimed it was actually 1990. The officer asked Manziel to empty his pockets. Upon examination the officer discovered Manziel's wallet held two additional identifications – one authentic, one fake. This brought the total number of identifications found on the person of Johnathan Manziel, future Heisman winner, to three.

The officer placed Manziel under arrest.

While Manziel was being lowered into the rear seat of a College Station police car, a witness told officers on the scene what actually happened. According to the witness, Manziel and a twenty year old male (later identified as Manziel's roommate and close friend Stevan Brant) were walking on the same sidewalk as the 47-year old man. As they passed one another, an inebriated Brant made an alleged racial slur in the direction of the African-American. The understandably enraged man confronted Brant about his choice of words. As the two men screamed at each other, Manziel stepped between the two in an attempt to play peacemaker. Apologizing on behalf of Brant, Manziel assured the older man he was taking his roommate home. This was not satisfactory for the 47-year old man. He shoved Manziel and punches were thrown.

Once booked, Manziel was charged with three state misdemeanors – Failure to Identify to Police, Possessing a Fake Driver's License and Disorderly Conduct. The resulting mug shot of a shirtless Manziel became internet fodder months later when the spotlight of fame found the Aggies' quarterback.

Fourteen months from his arrest and two days before his Media Days appearance, Manziel entered Judge Dana Zachary's courtroom to resolve the pending case. Dressed in a blue dress shirt, jeans, and an A&M maroon wristband, Manziel pled guilty to the stiffest of the three charges – Failure to Identify to Police. The plea agreement negotiated by Manziel's attorney Cam Reynolds ordered the quarterback to pay $2232 in fines and court costs, plus two days in jail. The incarceration punishment was window dressing as Manziel's night in city lockup was accepted as credit for the two day sentence. The agreement allowed Manziel to avoid a possible 180 days in jail.

"Johnny took responsibility for his actions that night and is ready to put what happened behind him," Reynolds said. "He didn't have to spend another second in jail. This case was never set for trial. He's ready to focus on the season and what is ahead of him."

In a move that echoed Manziel's playing style, the hearing, originally scheduled for later in the afternoon, was covertly moved to the morning. Media, in town to report on the plea agreement, was not notified. Much like a defensive end's grasp that Manziel routinely spins out of, the assembled press was left empty handed.

Johnny Manziel had warned the public relations staff, weeks in advance, that his plea agreement for the June 2012 arrest would be resolved roughly 48 hours before he hit the Wynfrey Hotel lobby. Working within the athletic department at Texas A&M, the staff had staged a series of meetings that prepared Manziel for the expected fallout. A confidence was building that the increasingly media-savvy quarterback would be able to gracefully fall upon his sword once the camera's light turned red.

This well-crafted plan was blown apart, two days before his plea agreement and four days before his Media Days appearance, by a late breaking ESPN report that Manziel had been asked to leave his job as a coach at the Manning Passing Academy. Citing sources that said Manziel missed practices and planning sessions for the camp, ESPN reported allegations that Manziel's dismissal was caused by late night drinking and the resulting hangover.

Work done far in advance of SEC Media Days was trashed as the tone of Manziel's upcoming interviews were about to drastically change. The public relations staff immediately went into damage control. The first call went to Manziel. They needed to know exactly what happened.

Those who feel Manziel lacks the character and maturity to succeed as a professional quarterback point to his departure from the Manning Passing Academy as proof he cannot be trusted. Extended over three nights and three mornings every year in July, the camp is the brainchild of the Manning family. The father, Archie, a former NFL star and his sons, current

NFL legends Peyton and Eli, oversee and run the camp from the football facilities of Nicholls State University in Thibodaux, Louisiana. The selling point of the annual camp is that the budding 13-18 year old quarterback in your family can come to a place where he will be instructed by some of the nation's best college quarterbacks, quarterback coaches, and even the Manning's. Having a Heisman winner such as Manziel was a huge draw for the passing academy. With pride they could tell the young passers that Manziel had attended the camp twice during his time at Kerrville Tivy High School.

That pride began to vanish on the first morning of the camp, as Manziel was running late. After missing most of the early coaching sessions with his assigned group of campers, Manziel finished the day and was asked to hang around to discuss his tardiness with an unnamed camp official. Confronted with Twitter pictures taken at pre-camp parties where alcohol was clearly visible, Manziel was reprimanded and told to return on time the next morning.

The following day, a Saturday, Manziel was nowhere to be found. Word trickled down to camp officials that Manziel had overslept and was feeling ill. This is what Manziel claimed once he was located. The Manning camp higher-ups, including Archie, responded with irritation and exhaustion. Several reports claimed Archie was the one to tell Manziel that he was excused from his counselor duties. This claim would later be denied by Manning spokesperson, Greg

Blackwell.   Regardless of who held the hatchet, Manziel was heading back to College Station.

Once ESPN broke the story and created a permanent location on their 24/7 ticker devoted to updated rumors as to what occurred, both the Manning's and Manziel's rushed to provide explanation. In the race to clarify, both camps only created a deeper sense that there was far more to the story than was being reported.

"After missing and being late for some practice assignments, Johnny explained that he had been feeling ill," Blackwell issued in an online statement. "Consequently, we agreed it was in everyone's best interest for him to go home a day early."

Manziel's father, Paul, texted a reporter from the Dallas Morning News that Johnny was "resting and recuperating from dehydration." This explanation died on the vine several hours later when Twitter photos and posts surfaced showing Manziel out at a local College Station bar at 1:30 in the morning.

The shady dismissal and ugly plea agreement made Manziel a punching bag in the first few non-A&M sessions at SEC Media Days. When McCarron was asked about his relatively quiet offseason in comparison to the endless joyride Manziel seemed to take pleasure in, the Alabama quarterback tightened his eyes and said, "My job is to play football. Not be a celebrity." If that didn't adequately eviscerate the public image of Johnny Football then Clowney's response to the question regarding his summer mantra did. Clowney's answer of "stay out of trouble" was followed with an inquiry as to how the potential number one pick in the NFL draft accomplished just that. "Stay off of Twitter," Clowney replied. "I don't know why people tweet crazy things. Everybody is going to see what you tweet." Johnny Football's 400,000 Twitter followers hoped the quarterback would ignore Clowney's unsolicited advice.

The swirling quagmire of Manziel's personal life moved ESPN SEC guru Paul Finebaum to state that the three hour inquisition the Aggie quarterback was about to undergo as "the biggest moment in the history of SEC Media Days." The ESPN interview, televised live on the network's Sports Center, failed to push Manziel to places he was not prepared to go. As he did the rest of the day, Manziel implored that he overslept and was not hung over the morning he went AWOL. He continued to dodge the question of whether he drank alcohol in Louisiana.

Roughly an hour after he first arrived to the Wynfrey, Manziel entered the main ballroom for his largest press conference of the day. Armed with recorders, iPhones, and iPads, the two hundred reporters mashed themselves against one another, registering Manziel's responses to seventy questions. Topics ranged from Manning camp to his college class load to Tim Tebow. The 31 minute question and answer session was the highlight of the Manziel televised flogging.

The quarterback was poised, relaxed, and direct with his responses. He would smile when needed, show an understanding of the gravity of his role as A&M quarterback when warranted, and elicit laughter from the collected press when he compared his concentrated media attention to the paparazzi that swarms Justin Bieber on a daily basis. "The spotlight is ten times brighter and ten times hotter than I thought it was two months ago," Manziel said during the press conference. With elegance, he exposed nothing that spoke to the rebellion many perceived to be swirling inside the soul of Johnny Football.

With congratulations and handshakes, Manziel and A&M head coach Kevin Sumlin boarded a plane to Los Angeles. Their destination, ESPN's annual award show the ESPY's, would serve as the final lap on the victory tour of Manziel's record-breaking 2012. The quarterback, scheduled to receive the trophy for Best College Athlete, began to feel the weight of his oppressions lift as the plane reached a cruising altitude over Texas. He was looking forward to the ceremony and the opportunities provided when the cultures of celebrity and athlete intertwined.

He was one of them now, a person who had everything in his life upended by fame. Functions such as the ESPY's gave Manziel a chance to seek advice on how to handle a life under the lights.

Manziel slowly worked the red carpet before the show, graciously accepting praise for his Heisman season and his performance at Media Days. Believing the worst was behind him, relief settled within the quarterback. "No more talk after this," Manziel said. "Let's play football."

It would not be that easy for Manziel. The same network honoring the quarterback was about to drop a bombshell.

It was news that would jeopardize everything.

3 ESPN

Even though media obligations before the start of fall training camp had ended for Johnny Manziel, Texas A&M head coach Kevin Sumlin could not partake in the same luxury. On the Tuesday after the conclusion of SEC Media Days, a day Sumlin would rather be back in College Station in preparation or relaxation, he was instead in Bristol, Connecticut. The small northeastern town is home to the studios of ESPN where a multitude of channels produce hundreds of hours of original programming every day.

Sumlin was in Bristol to endure what is affectionately referred to as the "ESPN Car Wash." With constant demand for content it is common for ESPN to invite or accept a visiting coach or player, or even a movie star willing to promote a new film, and run them from set to set filling their morning with interview after interview. Sumlin's visit would encompass four shows over three networks in the span of five hours. He bounced from the ESPN2 morning show "First Take" to the ESPNU studio and their daily show "College Game Day." He followed those two stops with two interviews on ESPN – one on "Sports Center" and another on "College Football Live."

Questions about Manziel's maturity and the distraction of his celebrity status were posed to Sumlin on set after set. Carrying the tone of a protective father, the A&M head coach was forthcoming in discussing Johnny's awkward walk into manhood. "The best thing I think that happened was us bringing him to SEC Media Days," said Sumlin. "Having him see the kind of questions and scrutiny that he's under and having to answer those questions for himself for three hours and see it for what it really is…I guarantee you, when he saw all those people and all those cameras, it hit him."

What struck Manziel, after Sumlin's layover in Bristol, was a profile in ESPN's biweekly magazine nakedly laying open the demons of Johnny Football. Written by Wright Thompson, the profile was a fair, nuanced portrait of a child struggling to become a man. Shadowing Manziel on a day where he shared a round of golf with his father, the reader is treated to a first person account of the tumultuous life the quarterback was thrust into after the Heisman. Nothing was off limits in Thompson's piece as the curtain was drawn on Manziel's alleged drinking, his impulsive posts on Twitter, and the increasing paranoia invading the quarterback and his family.

Manziel did not enter this post-Heisman world blindly. Late in 2012, as the A&M quarterback rode through a parade of celebratory Heisman interviews, the newly crowned Aggie visited former ESPN host Dan Patrick's radio show. In the midst of their conversation, Patrick stepped outside his role of interviewer and offered Manziel prudent advice. "Prepare yourself because people are going to come after you," Patrick said. In the successive weeks as Patrick's prophecy became reality, Manziel found it particularly difficult to reconcile the lacerating jabs thrown his way. The detractors, the haters, and the anonymous internet barkers all tore at Manziel's fragile, still developing sense of self.

As a result he became defensive. He clung to the immediacy of Twitter because he could respond first hand to the biting comments. His parents, also feeling attacked, defended themselves and their son on popular Aggie message boards. The push to respond did little to stop the endless waves of slander. Instead it irritated a fracture aching to heal.

Suffocating Manziel was the doubt of others. He felt at every difficult junction in his football career that people believed his talent and success was temporary. The hounding insecurity drove Manziel to accept Thompson's request for an all access interview. The writer effortlessly linked Manziel's inability to shrug off the flood of harmful opinions to Johnny's well publicized bouts of public self-destruction.

If Manziel granted the interview to stem the tide of hate, and open the door to sympathy, then he miscalculated the acidic nature of those who detested him. On the heels of the Manning Camp debacle, the plea agreement, and the resulting stream of negative publicity, the Thompson profile fed the notion Manziel was running head first into disaster. A conclusion that would undoubtedly cost Texas A&M their best chance at a national title in decades, and on a personal level destroy Johnny's chance at a lucrative NFL career.

The only true weapon Manziel held in the fight for his soul was to put together a second season that forced his non-believers to admire the depth and spectacular nature of his talent. Manziel did not need their love but he demanded their respect. The hope he could do this in peace vanished when an NCAA investigation created a vacuum where Manziel had no idea if that day's practice would forever be his last in College Station.

A handful of days after Alabama destroyed Notre Dame in the BCS championship game, the NCAA quietly began an official inquiry into a possible rule violation by Johnny Manziel. Sparking the investigation was the sudden emergence of numerous autographed items by Manziel on the popular auction website Ebay.com. The NCAA investigators became even more intrigued by the claim that all of the items had been authenticated and were being offered by a single autograph dealer.

The explosion of the sports autographs market had forced the NCAA to step up efforts to monitor the internet for signed items from amateur athletes. The rule in question, NCAA bylaw 12.5.2.1, stated that no athlete participating in NCAA sponsored events could autograph a large number of items they knew would then be offered for commercial sale. If the NCAA could find a trail that led back to Manziel, and discover proof of his knowledge that these items were headed to Ebay, then the A&M quarterback would be subject to disciplinary action. Additionally, if they found Manziel had accepted payment for the autographs, a greater punishment waited, and his eligibility to participate in A&M's upcoming football season would be at risk.

Over the next several months, investigators attempted to build a case against Manziel. Beginning with the autograph dealer offering the lion's share of autographed items, the NCAA asked on several occasions for an interview. The dealer refused. He did not have to comply because the NCAA lacked subpoena power to force a witness' testimony. Further attempts to gather even a rudimentary level of evidence against Manziel came up empty. The flailing investigation was dead in the water.

What resurrected the investigation was the diligent reporting of ESPN investigative reporter Darren Rovell. After news of the stalled inquiry into Manziel leaked to Rovell, he retraced the path of the initial NCAA investigation with far greater persistence. Under the direction of Rovell the story exploded. On the ESPN show "Outside the Lines" Rovell detailed an alleged meeting between Manziel and an autograph broker out of Miami named Drew Tieman. According to Rovell, the meeting at Tieman's apartment was where Manziel signed hundreds of items for a pre-arranged five figure fee. In the early days of the NCAA investigation Tieman refused to speak, but when contacted by Rovell, the dealer sang like a canary.

Additional reports by Rovell alleged Manziel had met and autographed items for money on several occasions with several brokers across the country. The ESPN reporter later testified he witnessed playback of videos shot by a broker showing the A&M quarterback signing items. Those alleged videos, reportedly filmed without Manziel's knowledge, were never shown on ESPN.

NCAA investigators, frustrated by the lack of cooperation, hoped to convince the new brokers uncovered by Rovell, to speak on the record. The NCAA believed Manziel was guilty, and to take down the reigning Heisman Trophy winner would restore faith in an office battered by incompetence. There was justice to seek and integrity to uphold. It was this lack of self-awareness, this entrenched arrogance that would ultimately undermine their efforts.

With their head held defiantly high, the NCAA stepped into the sun and walked straight into an ambush that would further destabilize their weakening hold in the debate of athlete compensation.

The NCAA rulebook is roughly 600 pages in length and as thick as a metropolitan area phonebook. The hefty tome lays out what is and is not acceptable in the eyes of college athletics' governing body. Everything from recruiting, to academic requirements, to the allowable size of a university provided scoop of butter and jelly for an athlete's breakfast, is covered in the rulebook. Critics argue hypocrisy lies within these boundaries set forth by the NCAA. They maintain these laws keep college athletes bound to the role of indentured servant to exploit and use as the universities, conferences, and NCAA see fit. A few of these same critics looking upon the Johnny Manziel investigation believed the quarterback's case spoke to the central problem of the amateur athlete being denied the right to profit off of his own likeness. To prove their point, and start what they hoped would be a backlash leading to change; these outspoken few felt they needed a high profile case such as Manziel's coupled with an inciting connection to put this perceived hypocrisy on display for a nation to judge. Hours after the investigation became public, one of those harsh critics became a fire starter, when he discovered the fallacy that would soon put Johnny Manziel in the center of a considerable media debate.

Jay Bilas was the one who lit the match. Bilas, a popular college basketball analyst for ESPN and longtime advocate for an overhaul to compensation rules for college athletes, is by all regards an active watchdog to all NCAA decisions and activities. This monitoring included coverage of the official and authorized NCAA website. Before the investigation of Manziel became public, the website offered the user an opportunity to purchase football jerseys in the school and number of their choice. This practice has always come under complaint as the jerseys displayed on the central page of the website coincide with the most

41

popular current players and their respective jersey numbers. The NCAA, when presented with such scrutiny, contends that this is nothing more than an occurrence of chance. There is no correlation between the Texas A&M maroon #2 Adidas jerseys sold in local College Station stores at $64.95, and the maroon #2 Adidas jersey Manziel wears every Saturday, according to the NCAA.

Bilas laid waste to this long held position in several keystrokes. Acting on a tip sent to him, the former Duke University basketball player found a page on ShopNCAASports.com offering A&M maroon Adidas jerseys with the #2 on both sides and the word "football" on the back nameplate. "I hadn't seen that before," Bilas told Laken Litman and Steve Berkowitz of USA Today. "That's the equivalent of putting his last name on there because it's not like jerseys have the sport on the back. So clearly they were referring to Johnny Football."

Bilas then found the search bar in the upper right corner. He began to plug name after name into the website. What emerged blew a large hole in the NCAA's argument. As Bilas typed Jadeveon Clowney, Braxton Miller, A.J. McCarron, and Andy Murray, their replicated jerseys popped up for purchase with the correct number and school in a bevy of colors to choose from. Each search and the corresponding screenshot were posted for public consumption on Bilas' Twitter account. "They're selling their jerseys, pretending that it is some sort of coincidence that all the value is in the school name and there's no value in

42

the player when coincidentally, every time you see a jersey, it's the team's best player," Bilas said. "It's not about need. It's about exploitation. Any time an entity or a person makes money off of another person, while at the same time restricting that person or entity, that's exploitation. It's wrong to the point of being immoral."

The backlash was swift and voluminous. Twitter became scorched earth as posters tweeted disgust at the NCAA hypocrisy. Columnists littered front pages with scathing editorials. It was a public relations nightmare that knocked the NCAA into a perception of being untrustworthy corporate oppressors.

The search function was disabled from the NCAA website in the hours after Bilas ignited the anger. "I can't speak to why we entered into that business," NCAA president Mark Emmert said. "It's not appropriate for us. There's no particularly compelling reason why the NCAA ought to be reselling jerseys from institutions."

As the NCAA spent time repairing their increasingly damaged public image, Texas A&M and the Manziel family sharpened their blades. If this was to become a war of attrition then both parties wanted experienced soldiers to exhaust the NCAA. The university struck first, hiring the law firm of Lightfoot, Franklin and White to thoroughly investigate the allegations against Manziel. The Alabama based firm gained notoriety in the wake of Cam Newton's eligibility investigation during his one year at Auburn.

The university and Newton won the case due to the contributions and steadfast defense provided by the firm, work that ultimately saved the national championship season for Auburn. After the high profile win, Lightfoot, Franklin and White were considered the best law firm in America for handling eligibility cases.

The Manziel's did not hesitate to hire someone who also had experience dealing with the NCAA. El Paso based lawyer Jim Darnell, who previously represented Baylor University and the University of Southern California, was hired to represent the quarterback's interest in the on-going investigation.

Johnny needed to push away the business of hiring lawyers. He had spent a summer putting in hours of preparation for the 2013 season, and regardless of the rumors that swirled around him, he knew to keep his sanity he would have to continue to punch the time clock every day. As camp opened, Manziel dissolved into the familiarity of throwing the football again and again.

He was not alone. Sure he had his teammates to lean on, but they had little to offer Manziel in the way of advice when dealing with the controversy. Johnny reached out to none other than Lebron James. The basketball icon knew a thing or two about how to deal with adversity. In the wake of his controversial decision to leave Cleveland for Miami, James watched as countless fans from Ohio burned his jersey, renounced their belief in him as a quality human being, and took to the internet to post death threats. He knew what it was like to live in the cocoon and his texts kept Manziel focused on what this season meant for his future.

With lawyers retained and Manziel distracted by football, the university unleashed an offensive against the reporter responsible for the renewed investigation. Troubled by the portrayal of Manziel in Rovell's ESPN reports, Texas A&M Chancellor John Sharp loudly voiced his displeasure in the way Johnny was being treated. In a tersely worded letter issued to members of his Chancellor's Century Council, Sharp denounced what he considered to be hostile abuse of A&M's starting quarterback by ESPN. "Darren Rovell of ESPN, who broke this story, has been duped before. During his report on Johnny Manziel, he cites unnamed sources who refuse to provide an interview or any tangible proof. In fact, his 'named source' Drew Tieman (initially referred to as the broker) was reportedly booked twice for possession of marijuana and placed on four years' probation. He has taken down his Facebook page, changed his telephone number and is refusing attempts to be interviewed by the NCAA. It is surprising that the nation's largest sports channel would support publication with this lack of corroboration," Sharp wrote to members. ESPN responded with a standard issue quote of "we stand by our reporting."

"There's zero doubt in my mind that Johnny Manziel is innocent," Sharp told Maggie Kiely of College Station's newspaper the *Eagle*. "He's a lot nicer than I am, I don't think I would have handled it as well as he has. None of us would want our sons to go through what he's had to."

The week that decided Manziel's fate began with a gesture of contempt. Perhaps worn thin by answering numerous questions about the A&M quarterback, SEC coaches got their revenge by laughably voting Manziel to their preseason All-SEC second team. Manziel, the reigning SEC offensive player of the year was beat out by Georgia's quarterback Andy Murray.

SEC coaches were not the only ones tiring of Manziel. One week before the home opener against Rice, weary NCAA investigators came to College Station to interview the Aggie quarterback. With Darnell by his side, Manziel answered questions for more than six hours. Throughout the conversation, the quarterback was steadfast in his denial that he had ever accepted money for his signature.

The interview was a means to an end. Without the power to subpoena, the NCAA had no witnesses to the alleged meetings. Without the testimony of those brokers and dealers that later spoke to ESPN's Rovell, there was a noticeable lack of evidence. And without anything credible to prove Manziel's guilt, the NCAA had only one card to play. They threatened Manziel and Texas A&M with stalling their investigation under the pretense they could use the time to convince those mute witnesses to somehow find the words.

The move was a despicable bluff. Once Chancellor Sharp voiced his belief that Manziel was innocent and being bullied by ESPN, the NCAA investigation was essentially neutered. The NCAA was merely the police. In principle, they would gather the evidence of wrong doing and then bring their findings to men like Sharp, whose job it was to then play executioner. But everything falls apart if the hatchet man believes the criminal is free of guilt. This was the dilemma facing the NCAA. Stubborn to walk away without even the smallest victory, the NCAA offered to complete their investigation and accept Manziel's version of the events with a simple caveat.

Manziel would have to accept a suspension.

Seventy-two hours before the Aggies kicked off their 2013 season, the decision on Manziel's punishment was announced. In a jointly issued statement, Texas A&M University and the NCAA agreed "that there is no evidence that quarterback Johnny Manziel received money in exchange for autographs" but "due to an inadvertent violation regarding the signing of certain autographs" the A&M signal caller was declared ineligible. However, if Manziel completed two conditions he would immediately be reinstated by the governing body. The lesser of the two stipulations held the obligation of addressing his teammates "regarding the situation and lessons learned." The second penalty was far more punitive. The A&M quarterback would serve a two quarter suspension in the upcoming game against Rice.

The statement and punishment was the result of hours of negotiation between the lawyers hired weeks before when all parties lunged for protection. The NCAA, pleased to get their pound of Manziel flesh, continued to trumpet their diligence in preserving amateurs. The announcement did little to stem the tide of distrust that seemed to be swallowing the NCAA. "Now Johnny Manziel can finally get back to his NCAA approved purpose," tweeted Andy Staples, the Sports Illustrated college football writer. "Selling jerseys for Adidas and Texas A&M."

The elation in the soft punishment for Manziel and the university was mutually shared. He would be on the gridiron in two weeks when Alabama visited Kyle Field. By that single standard, the settlement was a success.

If there was a winner in the autograph scandal, it was ESPN. The network reaped a goldmine of interest as Manziel was held in limbo. When Saturday arrived and Johnny was reduced to first-half cheerleader, ESPN was there to televise the game against Rice. The network was not shy in lingering on shots of Manziel wearing a visor, towel wrapped around his neck, celebrating the four first half touchdowns A&M scored without his assistance. As the first half ended, ESPN had shown Manziel on thirty-three separate occasions.

The eager Manziel was the first to enter the locker room sprinting far ahead of his jogging teammates. The sold-out crowd cheered as the remaining Aggies leisurely made their way off the field. Some of those standing and applauding were vocal about their disgust for the Johnny Football circus. And now, twenty minutes from his return, the question remained – how many of them would be cheering when it was Manziel's turn to play?

4 Rice & SHSU

The frustration of living under the narrowing microscope in College Station came to a tipping point in the early morning hours of a Sunday in June 2013. Fishing on the Texas coast with teammates, Johnny Manziel received a call around midnight from his roommate. The roommate did not want to talk, but the police did. A College Station officer told Manziel his car was parked the wrong way on the street in front of his house. There were two options – move the car or receive a ticket. Manziel asked for leniency from the officer as he had the only set of keys, a couple of hundred miles away on the Gulf of Mexico. The incident, silly and mundane, was worth barely a mention. What made it a story was how Manziel reacted. He took to Twitter and fired off an incendiary tweet about the town where he lived.

@JManziel2:

Bullshit like tonight is a reason why I can't wait to leave College Station...whenever it may be.

The Manziel's believed the call was an invasion of privacy. "They know where Johnny lives," Paul Manziel, Johnny's father told ESPN's Wright Thompson. "They take him home after games. They know whose car it is. They are harassing him." But for citizens of College Station, the individuals who lived for Saturdays at Kyle Field, the comment was not appreciated. They pounded Manziel's Twitter feed with unrestrained rage. The quarterback disposed of the offending remarks quickly, but the damage was done.

Anger directed at Manziel grew intense after the tweet that began the A&M quarterback's disorderly summer. Letters laced with disgust poured into the editor's office at the *Eagle*. One man called Manziel "classless." Another was furious Manziel hadn't responded to his request for an autograph. And finally, an avid Aggie fan called the quarterback "a disgrace to himself, his family, his team, his coaching staff and Texas A&M University." When faced with these direct attacks, Manziel was unapologetic. "I probably rubbed people the wrong way in some cases. But at the end of the day, people are mad at me and upset with me because I'm doing everything they want to do," the embattled quarterback told Andy Staples, Sports Illustrated's college football writer.

Manziel didn't have to apologize to the city of College Station, but he did have to make that gesture to his teammates. On the eve of the season opener, after mandatory team meetings, the 2013 Texas A&M football team gathered to hear Manziel fulfill the first stipulation required to regain his eligibility. The speech, about the lessons he had learned over the odyssey of the past several weeks, satisfied the initial requirement of his suspension but Manziel chose to go deeper with his words. Looking onto the faces that made the seventh ranked team in the country, their starting quarterback implored his old, and new, teammates to trust in the work they put in over the spring and summer months. Together they had bonded and grown in ways that made him proud. Do not let anything break apart this bond, he urged. Not the media. Not the NCAA. No one. To his teammates, the ones that fed off his limitless energy, the expression of regret was unnecessary. "He's a fiery guy and that's what we love about him. He's not quiet. He's not shy," said A&M offensive tackle Cedric Ogbuehi. "He's going to be loud and aggressive and that's what makes him Johnny Football. We love it."

As the first half against Rice ended, it was the suspension plagued A&M defense that was asking for absolution. Missing several starters due to offseason legal problems, the Owls offense had gutted the Aggies for over 300 total yards and 21 first half points. If Matt Joeckel, the replacement starter at quarterback for A&M, had not found his rhythm in the second quarter then Manziel might have been returning to mount a second half comeback. Instead the Aggies held a delicate 28-21 lead. Electricity rippled through the sold out crowd as the Aggies disappeared into the tunnel leading to the locker room. They may not have been ready to forgive, but they were aching to see him play.

The halftime buzz became a deafening roar as the second half began with A&M senior cornerback Tramain Jacobs intercepting Rice's Taylor McHargue's pass to give A&M a first and ten on the Rice 40 yard line. An eager Manziel bounced onto the field slapping hands and helmets as the standing crowd chanted "Johnny! Johnny!" With adrenaline flooding heart and head, Manziel took his first snap of the season, dropped back to pass, missed an open receiver, tucked the football and ran. He slid through the crush of lineman and sped into the Rice secondary before being tackled at the Rice 28. The left, then right, twelve yard run was followed with a seven yard scramble. Unfortunately for Manziel, an incompletion and sack derailed the excitement as A&M settled for a 44 yard field goal. The three points pushed the Aggie lead to ten.

Any residual disappointment from the opening drive was wiped away moments later when A&M junior safety Clay Honeycutt stepped in front of another McHargue pass and returned the turnover to the Owls' 34 yard line. The second consecutive interception provided Manziel another golden opportunity for his first touchdown. He would not spoil the chance as the quarterback connected with his favorite target from 2012, the redshirt sophomore Mike Evans, for a 23 yard touchdown. Manziel raced to the end zone and celebrated by jumping and colliding in mid-air with the wide receiver. The lead was now 38-21 in A&M's favor and the rout was officially on.

With the game unraveling, the lone remaining mystery was to see if Manziel could make it through the rest of the game without incident. The Heisman, the Manning camp debacle, and the autograph investigation, had clearly made Manziel a prime target for opponent abuse. On several occasions, during his brief appearance against Rice, defenders placed themselves inches away from the A&M quarterback's facemask. Some exchanges were idle chatter, but at other times Manziel was smacked with vicious, stinging barbs. The quarterback had been warned, by Sumlin and other coaches on the A&M staff, that the acid thrown by opposing teams would serve one sole purpose – to disrupt the focus lying within Manziel. To appear upset, or worse, react to the taunting, would only assure that teams would be diligent in trying to rattle his cage for the rest of the season.

The jawing came to a head moments after Manziel completed his second touchdown to Evans. Amid the end zone celebration, the quarterback became locked in a verbal altercation with Rice safety Malcolm Hill. The two exchanged heated words, leading an official to step between Manziel and Hill in an effort to diffuse the situation. Manziel then mimicked an autograph and pointed to the scoreboard. The latter gesture, considered taunting by the NCAA, prompted the official to throw his flag and penalize A&M fifteen yards for unsportsmanlike conduct.

Manziel's behavior and subsequent penalty enraged Sumlin. The head coach ran to meet his quarterback and launched into a profanity laced tirade when Manziel crossed the sideline. Manziel never stopped, bumping into Sumlin on the way to the bench. He removed his helmet and sat down. There was little need for him to prepare for A&M's next offensive possession; Sumlin had let Manziel know his day was done.

The final score read Aggies 52, Owls 31. In roughly twenty minutes of play Manziel completed six of eight passes and threw for three touchdowns. Not a soul in the media cared. Manziel, Sumlin, and officials at Texas A&M all agreed, in the weeks leading to the Rice game, there was little to be gained from the quarterback addressing the media. Therefore, the responsibility of explaining what happened in the moments following the taunting penalty fell upon the head coach. Denying that Manziel's refusal to stop and listen to his coach's berating was disrespectful, Sumlin acknowledged the benching of his quarterback was due to the penalty. "When (Manziel) came off the field, I made two statements to him, neither one of which he should have responded to," said Sumlin. "They weren't questions. They were direct statements that I can't repeat right now." Laughter erupted from the surrounding journalists. The head coach did not share their joyous nature.

Sumlin was insulted by the snowballing opinion that he was at the helm of a program in disarray. Instead of concentrating on football, the A&M head coach was being forced to address the

55

mounting evidence that suspensions, off-season arrests, and the reckless behavior of Manziel, were undermining the hope that the 2013 season would be played to potential. If the head coach is underrated at anything it is his ability to handle the media. With wide dark eyes accompanied by arching eyebrows that start high and dive toward the bridge of his nose, Sumlin can float effortlessly from humor to sternness. "For people to say, 'Hey, do you know what? (Manziel's) not listening to his coach and there's no discipline in this program, they're not around this football team. They are not around this program," Sumlin said.

Sumlin wanted to change the conversation because the week two game against Sam Houston State was undeniably important. The Bearkats had been to back to back FCS Championship games, the division directly below Texas A&M, where a single elimination tournament determined it champion. Several Aggies believed the team could not look ahead to next week's game against Alabama.

"If you don't come out, this team will come out and beat you," Texas A&M running back Ben Malena said. "We know that we have to prepare this week and we have to be ready for them. They have to be ready for them. They have some great players, some former Division I players. They have some great talent. You can't overlook schools. We have to prepare for them like they're a conference opponent."

For Manziel the game would be a chance to accumulate repetitions with his offense. Against Rice, the quarterback only had five possessions with the first team. In addition, the Sam Houston contest would allow the swirling madness around Manziel to settle, a process Sumlin was fully aware needed to happen.

"Anybody who watches Johnny knows he plays with a lot of passion and emotion," Sumlin said. "Because of that he gets into a grey area. As coaches, it's our job to keep that energy going but keep it positive. What you don't want to do is kill that passion, because it separates Johnny from a lot of players."

Sam Houston's strategy on the defense was to confuse Manziel by mixing their coverages. On most plays, the Bearkats dropped eight defenders creating a far reaching and extended zone. At other times, Sam Houston would show the zone but send an all-out blitz. Neither was particularly effective, as Manziel completed ten of his first fourteen passes for 154 yards. The quarterback shined late in the first quarter, leading A&M on a 75 second touchdown drive with his 27 yard strike to Sabian Holmes, giving the Aggies a 14-7 lead.

While the A&M defense found their rhythm, forcing four straight punts, Manziel continued to pick apart the Sam Houston zone. The quarterback converted all three third downs he faced as the Aggie offense started the second quarter with a 90 yard touchdown drive giving A&M a 21-7 lead. Two drives later, the A&M quarterback had moved the football 50 yards in six plays but when challenged with a third and nine on Sam Houston's 20 yard line, Manziel made his most confident pass. Taking the snap, the A&M quarterback tossed a floating pass that reached wide receiver Ja'Quay Williams in stride. Williams caught the throw for a touchdown to push the A&M lead to 27-7. After Sam Houston and Texas A&M traded final scoring drives, the teams headed to the locker room with the Aggies on top, 30-14. Manziel was ridiculous in the first half completing 23 of 32 passes for 326 yards.

Sam Houston started the second half by exposing the inexperience of A&M's defense. Bearkat running back Timothy Flanders received a third down pitch, turned the corner and raced down the sideline for a 68 yard touchdown. The run became possible when the A&M defensive end responsible for edge containment on the play, bounced to the inside leaving Flanders a wide path to the outside. The touchdown closed the lead to nine, 30-21.

Manziel owned the first half because the Bearkats only rushed three defenders on the majority of plays. Against one of the best offensive lines in college football, Sam Houston forfeited the chance to put pressure on the A&M quarterback. Led by consensus All-American left tackle Jake Matthews, the Aggies' front line would not surrender a sack all evening. Without being hurried, Manziel converted nine of eleven third downs in the first and second quarters. Success continued on the opening drive of half number two as Manziel completed a 12 yard third down pass to Evans moving the ball to Sam Houston State's 35 yard line. Six straight rushes led to Tra Carson's second touchdown of the game. The lead was back to sixteen.

After the wobbly A&M defense settled and forced their fifth punt of the game, Manziel went back to work. He started the drive with a deep completion to Evans for 42 yards. Three plays later, he found Brandon Williams alone in the end zone for a ten yard touchdown reception. The A&M sideline began to breathe a little easier as the extra point made the score Texas A&M 44, Sam Houston State 21. With only six and a half minutes left in the third quarter, the coaches began to discuss how much longer Manziel would remain in the game.

The conversation was dropped in mid-sentence as Bearkat quarterback Brian Bell connected with wideout Torrance Williams. Sam Houston's speedy senior receiver outran the A&M secondary crossing the goal line 75 yards from the line of scrimmage. The Bearkat home run cut the lead to sixteen and more importantly once again made the game a two possession contest. Sam Houston State's head coach Willie Fritz, not believing his defense could stop Manziel, tried to keep momentum on the Bearkats side by attempting an onside kick. The Aggies weren't fooled as they easily recovered the live football at the Bearkats' 46 yard line.

Manziel started his final drive of the game with 6:13 left in the third quarter. Two monster rushes by the senior Malena gave the A&M offense a first and goal at Sam Houston's six yard line. Manziel took the next snap, looked for an open receiver and fled from the collapsing pocket. Bearkat cornerback Shelby Davis left his assignment and met the Aggie quarterback near the goal line creating a collision that saw Davis bowled over by Manziel. The Manziel touchdown run ignited the sellout crowd into a sustained roar. The quarterback's final play of the night made the score 51-28, Aggies.

Manziel was no longer needed because on the next drive A&M linebacker Nate Askew intercepted a Bell pass and returned it 30 yards for a touchdown. The lead was now 30 points and it was safe for Manziel to trade his helmet for visor.

As the clock reached zero and the two teams left their respective sidelines to shake hands, reporters surrounded Manziel. He had not spoken to the press since that long, torturous morning at SEC Media Days and as a concession Sumlin had agreed to let Manziel address reporters after the game. It was a calculated move by the A&M head coach. He wasn't going to allow anyone access to his starting quarterback over the next several days. He wanted Manziel focused on Alabama. Tonight was the media's lone chance to tackle the topics left unanswered in the weeks leading to the season.

When asked what helped get Manziel through the tumultuous days of August, when his eligibility hung in the balance, the quarterback did not hesitate to give credit. "The biggest thing that's helped has just been being around these guys, being in this building, having my teammates," Manziel said. "It makes it easy to block all this stuff out and grow with my teammates and build a bond with them. That's what's been most helpful." The quarterback torched the Bearkats with 403 yards in the air, 36 yards by land, and 4 total touchdowns. His favorite target, Mike Evans, caught seven of those throws for 155 yards. Their connection was the most explosive weapon at A&M offensive coordinator Clarence McKinney's disposal.

After the press conference, Manziel showered and packed his bag. The College Station police escorted the quarterback home where he soon fell asleep, with his mind swimming in thoughts about the week ahead. He could relax, comforted by the fact that he would not have to leave, Alabama was coming to him.

The "Game of the Century" was a week away.

5 Alabama

The last time a game meant this much College Station was awash in grief. On November 26th, 1999, eight days after a student built bonfire collapsed, killing twelve young Aggies, the University of Texas traveled to Kyle Field for their annual rivalry game against a heavy-hearted Texas A&M team. In a football game that had little consequence on where the two teams were headed in the postseason, hope existed the contest would provide the first step in healing.

During the somber game, tributes were made to the fallen. Twelve doves were set free moments before kickoff. At halftime, the Longhorns' band raised the colors of Texas A&M, maroon and white, and performed a haunting version of Amazing Grace. On a day filled with remembrances, the one paid by the A&M football team that Saturday was perhaps the greatest and most needed of them all.

Tight throughout, the Aggies found themselves down three late in the fourth quarter. The quarterback of the 1999 A&M team, Randy McCown, led a drive deep into Texas territory that gave A&M an opportunity to take an improbable lead. From the Longhorns' 15 yard line, McCown connected with wide receiver Matt Bumgardner on a touchdown pass, sending the largest crowd ever to witness a Texas football game into delirium.

Pressed by a dwindling clock, Texas, down by four points, threatened to spoil the upset. Major Applewhite, the Longhorns' quarterback, raced Texas within striking distance of a game winning touchdown.

It was here the Aggies took a chance.

Hoping to cause a momentum swinging play, the call was made to send A&M cornerback Jay Brook on a blitz. As Applewhite dropped in the pocket, the Aggie defensive back reached him before he could throw the football. Brook walloped the Longhorns' passer, causing the ball to pop loose. A mad, impassioned scramble for the football created a pile that took referees considerable time to sort through.

On the bottom, with both arms around the football was A&M linebacker Brian Gamble. When Gamble emerged, with his recovery held high, the crowd erupted into sobbing, electric delight. The linebacker dropped to his knees, let the football spill from his fingers, and raised his arms to the sky. "I wanted to thank the man upstairs," Gamble said. "I knew that he was looking down on us today. So were our classmates." The image of Gamble thanking the heavens, moments after securing the 20-16 A&M victory flooded Sunday newspapers across the country.

Fourteen years later, albeit in a far more jovial nature, a nation's eyes turned again to College Station.

Top ranked Alabama was in route to Kyle Field to play the sixth ranked Aggies of Texas A&M. The game would be a rematch of college football's best game from 2012, a barn burner that introduced the world to Johnny Football. The fanfare, the deluge of media, and the attention afforded the school and city was why A&M moved to the SEC.

For College Station, hosting the game meant dealing with the circus. The event, many considered to be the most important ever to be played at Kyle Field, brought over 120,000 spectators, twelve satellite trucks, five production trailers and three media buses to the city. Tickets to the game averaged $763 per seat, the highest price ever for a regular season college football game.

Games like the one to be played against the Crimson Tide were extremely bountiful to the participants. Close to ten million watched the A&M-Alabama game in 2012, a number that would certainly be surpassed in 2013. ESPN was bringing their popular College Game Day program to College Station with live broadcasts to begin on the Thursday before the game. CBS, responsible for broadcasting the game, made the rare decision to move their studio on site for their pregame show. Numerous radio outlets – Sirius XM, ESPN, and CBS – had taken over portions of the A&M campus to broadcast their programs. It was a bonanza for the school. "Where else can we get millions of people to watch a seven hour commercial about Texas A&M on a Saturday in the fall?" A&M senior athletics director Jason Cook said.

Students at A&M were not immune to "big game" fever. One male student posted a challenge to Twitter letting his followers know that if a post received over 10,000 retweets then he would streak across Kyle Field at some point during Saturday's game. 48 hours later, the dare had been retweeted more than 17,000 times. In addition to several marriage offers the student was called into A&M President R. Bowen Loftin's office and warned "to keep his clothes on and follow the rules."

Despite the potential for amusing hijinks, the possible streaker was not the A&M undergrad garnering the most attention during Alabama week. That honor was Johnny Manziel's to revel in after the quarterback was placed upon the cover of Time Magazine. It was a "wow" moment for those who spent their lives around college football. Manziel had transcended the sport and been lifted into the rarified air of national celebrity. "This is not football we're talking about," Finebaum said. "This is TMZ, this is National Enquirer, this is unique. With all due respect to Lebron (James), who's getting married, and Tiger Woods, who is struggling on the golf course, there have been more conversations about Johnny Manziel than any player in a long time."

CBS added to the fervor when Craig Silver, an executive in the sports division, told Richard Deitsch of Sports Illustrated, "no matter where (Manziel) is and no matter what part of the game it is, we will have a shot of it." News of a "Johnny-Cam" was not well received by Aggies head coach Kevin Sumlin.

Concerned that a live feed of Manziel could provide an advantage to A&M's future opponents, plus being leery at the message it sent to current A&M players not named Manziel, Sumlin asked for clarification and correction. "To me it's interesting," Sumlin said. "Everything we do here at Texas A&M is about team. It's about building our team, building our program and not being an individual. Saturday afternoon you're going to have two football teams on the field. I just don't understand why there's got to be one guy singled out with a camera on him the entire time. That's not what we're trying to be about. That's not what we're trying to promote and certainly from my standpoint looking out at all the criticism about individualism on a football team, I don't think this helps enhance the team concept one bit."

These were the annoyances and distractions burdened to football programs that mattered. Regardless of Sumlin's prickly demeanor, the head coach and school wouldn't want it any other way.

On November 10th, 2012, upon the hallowed field in Tuscaloosa, Alabama, Johnny Manziel became engraved in our forever. Spinning, ducking and flying "like a hummingbird on crystal meth," the quarterback led Texas A&M into Bryant-Denny Stadium and defeated No. 1 Alabama 29-24. This was the reason for the pomp and circumstance assembled in Aggieland. A country wanted to see if Manziel could do it again.

What was most startling about the 2012 upset was not necessarily *that* it happened but rather *how* it happened.   Striking first, then second, and after Alabama quarterback A.J. McCarron's midfield interception, the Aggies posted their third straight unanswered touchdown giving them a 20-0 first quarter lead.   An astounding figure when you consider Alabama only surrendered 26 points all season in the first quarter of their 2012 title run.

Manziel was brilliant in the opening stanza. By completing ten of eleven passes for 76 yards and rushing the football five times for 74 yards, the Aggie offense was able to post an astounding nine first downs in the opening quarter.

The loss did not derail Alabama from their third title in four years but the defeat cut wounds that continued to run deep. "They came out and attacked us and kind of hit us in the mouth and we didn't respond real well early," Alabama defensive coordinator Kirby Smart said. "As long as I've been here, I really don't remember a game quite like that." To underline the principle that losing is not tolerated within the institution of Alabama football, the game film from the A&M defeat was played continuously in the Alabama weight room over the spring and summer of 2013.

In preparation for the rematch against the Aggies, Alabama head coach Nick Saban zeroed in on ways to better contain Manziel. The free-wheeling style of the A&M quarterback went against the grain of everything the Alabama leader held to be true about championship football. Saban wanted large, beastly lineman on both sides of the football to wreak constant punishment, crippling an opponent in the third and fourth quarters. In Saban's dream, a strong, mistake free running game then takes over, allowing Alabama to control both clock and scoreboard.

Manziel and his ability to find the end zone in a mashed flurry of no-huddle hallucinations caused Saban great worry. Saban told Sports Illustrated in 2011, "even when you've called the right defense and your defense does everything right, that kind of quarterback can still beat you by improvising. It's the stuff you can't really plan for that always brings a high level of concern. I mean, it can drive you crazy as a coach."

Alabama's coaching staff began to prepare for Manziel in the spring. Saban hosted assorted staff from the NFL trying to find novel approaches to defending the read-option quarterbacks that flourished across the professional league in the fall of 2012. The knowledge culled from those symposiums was not passed to Crimson Tide players until the two week period they had to prepare for the Aggies. After Alabama looked vulnerable in their 2013 opener against Virginia Tech, a 35-10 win, Saban decided his team needed more not less. He put Alabama through two weeks of work similar to what the players experienced in August. "I think it needed to be a hard (off) week," Saban said. "I told the players that because I believe we need to improve. I think we can all be committed to doing more, capable of doing more in terms of commitment, discipline, being a good

68

teammate, caring for each other, preparing better for the game. You show what your desire is by what you do every day, and I think the players responded and did a really good job."

Considering the time Alabama had to prepare, the importance of the game, the work put forth, and remembrance of that wretched first quarter all those months ago, one had to believe the rematch would begin differently.

Instead, the Crimson Tide arrived in College Station, watched their opening kickoff soar into the air and forgot to protect their face as Manziel, once again, punched the Tide squarely between the eyes.

Johnny hounded the Alabama defense in the first quarter. On the opening play, Manziel danced two steps to the right then exploded left for a 12 yard run. The quarterback followed his keeper with a quick 32 yard lob to Mike Evans and two plays in, A&M sat at the Alabama 40. Two plays later, Manziel connected with Evans again, staying comfortable in a pocket well protected by his offensive line, for 35 yards. Two rushes by senior running back Ben Malena failed to cross the goal line, so on third down A&M offensive coordinator Clarence McKinney called for a play action pass. Manziel moved with Malena to the right, faked the exchange, turned to his left and floated a pass to the waiting recipient, tight end Cameron Clear. Seven plays covered the 84 yards in 2 minutes and 39 seconds. Manziel calmly returned to the sideline, accepting congratulations and water on the very hot afternoon. The extra point split the uprights. A&M led 7-0.

Alabama's attempt to counter the Aggies' score fell flat. Two false start penalties caused by the deafening Kyle Field crowd, known as the 12th Man, pushed the Crimson Tide from a second down and short to a second and long. The two plays that followed were weak, feeble efforts. Alabama's punter boomed a 55 yard kick out of his own end zone and Manziel returned to the field at the A&M 41 yard line.

Helpless to stop the velocity of the A&M offense, Saban and defensive coordinator Smart hoped to take away Manziel's most trusted target in wide receiver Evans. John Fulton, Alabama's starting right cornerback, was unsuccessful on the game's first drive as Evans had two catches for 67 yards. The Crimson Tide coaching duo believed backup sophomore Cyrus Jones might have more luck. After Manziel opened the drive with two rushes for 24 yards, Jones was tested. Under pressure, Manziel scrambled around, keeping the play alive far longer than it had any right to be. Jones failed to keep up with Evans as Manziel hit the wideout in stride for a 34 yard gain. Malena squeezed through the middle on the next play for a one yard touchdown and Alabama, reeling from the one-two combo of Manziel and Evans, was down 14-0.

Moments after the 2012 Aggies walked off the field at Cowboys Stadium, host to the Cotton Bowl,

the 2013 A&M defense received its' first hit. Six
starters from the defense had played their final game,
five were casualties of graduation and one entered the
NFL draft. Over an offseason where their quarterback
was the central focus of attention, three returning
A&M starters from the defense were arrested. Safety
Floyd Raven Jr. and cornerback Deshazor Everett were
charged with assault. Anchor of the defensive line,
tackle Kirby Ennis, was booked for disorderly conduct
and discharging a firearm. Suspensions for the trio
were handed down promptly. Ennis and Raven Jr.
were out for the entire Rice game and Everett missed
the first half. The final blow came minutes before the
Rice game, as the A&M athletic department issued a
one sentence statement informing the press that starting
cornerback DeVante Harris, linebacker Steven Jenkins,
and defensive end Gavin Stansbury were all suspended
for the first two games of the season.

Before the rash of suspensions, the returning
Aggies accounted for only 71 career starts. Taking
away those players forced to sit out, only two
defenders had ever started a game at A&M. The
reliance on inexperience plagued the Aggies against
Rice and Sam Houston. In 2012, only one team, LSU,
rushed for more than 200 yards against defensive
coordinator Mark Snyder's 4-3 defense. Both
opponents in 2013 had already eclipsed the 200 yard
threshold, with Rice running for 306 yards and Sam
Houston totaling over 240 on the ground. Relying
solely on true freshmen to fill the holes led to expected
mistakes. Poor angles on tackle attempts, missed

71

assignments, and stretches played in utter confusion were some of the lowlights the Aggie defense displayed over the first two games.

Struggling was a necessary thing for the freshmen the A&M defense was relying on. Snyder believed by failing and learning to correct basic mistakes, those players would add depth the Aggies could depend on in the foreseeable future. But make no mistake; Snyder and Kevin Sumlin were delighted to be at full strength for Alabama. "The familiarity and the experience factor of those guys coming back is going to help our confidence as a defense," Sumlin said. "The confidence in our coaches to be able to change the schemes and do some different things instead of being very vanilla, which we have been the last couple of weeks because of our youth."

Renewed self-assurance, blended with a howling 12th Man, had pushed Alabama's offense off the field on the Tide's first drive of the game. Abandoning the run temporarily, Saban put the second drive in senior quarterback A.J. McCarron's hands. He completed four throws on a drive that covered 75 yards. McCarron's 22 yard touchdown pass to wide receiver Kevin Norwood cut the A&M lead to seven.

A&M's attempt to answer Alabama's score was hampered by a botched kick return. Despite having to start the drive at their own two yard line, Manziel was able to move the Aggies into Alabama territory. A questionable offensive pass interference call against Evans ended any hope the push would be fruitful. The Aggies punted and the first quarter was over.

Mark Snyder's entire defensive philosophy revolves around getting off the field on third down and forcing the opponent to punt the football. So dedicated is Snyder he creates entire practices around the mantra. The coordinator's goal is to hold the offense to third down conversions less than 35% of the time. In 2012, the Aggies ranked fifth in the SEC surrendering a first down on third down 33% of the time. There was perhaps a glimmer of hope in the knowledge that this year's defensive unit, despite all the subtractions, was allowing a first down on just 39% of opportunities.

Two McCarron incompletions had created a third and ten for Alabama. Twice, the Tide quarterback looked to his primary target, the talented sophomore wideout Amari Cooper, without success. Looking unsettled with his first two throws, McCarron finally connected with Cooper on third down for 21 yards. Unable to stop the Tide on the long conversion allowed McCarron to set up Alabama's second touchdown.

Ten of Alabama's previous eleven plays had been pass calls. Appearing to abandon the run was not a rash overreaction to Manziel's early outburst, but rather a ploy to set up a home run. After moving to A&M's 44 yard line on the strength of a McCarron 15 yard completion, the call was made to take advantage of a leaning, inexperienced defense.

The Tide quarterback received the snap and handed the football to the running back, T.J. Yeldon. The sophomore lunged forward, stopped, then turned and pitched the ball back to McCarron. Racing down the left sideline was Tide wideout DeAndrew White. The flea-flicker had fooled Aggie safety, Howard Matthews, and allowed White an open path to the center of the field. McCarron unleased a rainbow that White caught for a game changing touchdown. The score was tied at 14.

In this media saturated culture we live in, it is essential for all Heisman winners to be able to point to one repeatable highlight that showcases their unique talent and convinces voters to place the player at the top of their ballot.

That unique play for Johnny Manziel came in the previous year's upset against Alabama.

On A&M's second drive of the 2012 game, leading 7-0 and already deep in Crimson Tide territory, Manziel received the shotgun snap and looked for a receiver in the end zone. With the pocket quick to break down, the quarterback looked to run. Bouncing right, Manziel pinballed directly into the back half of retreating right guard Cedric Ogbuehi. The collision forced the ball from Manziel's throwing hand and into the air. Alabama's secondary seeing the floating fumble "did what they shouldn't have done," said Alabama safety Vinnie Sunseri. "They came out of their zones. They didn't cover their man and it opened

74

up the middle of the field." Manziel snatched the football, spun to his left and in the face of the swarming Crimson Tide defense, threw a touchdown to the waiting A&M receiver Ryan Swope. "That (play) kind of made him the Heisman winner because every Heisman needs that one play, one game and I'm guessing that was it," Ogbuehi said.

The 2013 version of "that one play" came on A&M's first drive of quarter two. Starting at his own 25 yard line, Manziel did not encounter any resistance from the Crimson Tide defensive front seven, moving the football into Alabama's end of the field for the fourth straight time. The lone third down on the drive was a third and eight on Alabama's 34 yard line. After the exchange from center, Manziel became locked in the hands of Crimson Tide defensive end Jeoffery Pagan. A&M's elusive quarterback was able to wrench free from Pagan's grasp, spinning and backpedaling close to 25 yards behind the line of scrimmage. With fearsome Alabama linebacker C.J. Mosley bearing down on Manziel, the quarterback lofted a jump ball some 40 yards down the center of the field. Gathering under the pass was a group of maroon and white jerseys. Several made leaping attempts for the ball, but it was Aggie receiver Edward Pope that came down with the pass. In the play-by-play recount it simply lists "Manziel pass complete to Edward Pope for 12 yards," but that certainly did not do the insanely entertaining play justice.

What was not entertaining for Aggie fans was how the drive ended. Manziel pushed the offense into a goal-to-go situation at the seven yard line of Alabama. On first down the A&M quarterback kept the football on an option play for three yards to the four. Offensive coordinator Clarence McKinney called for what is arguably the worst play in football, the end zone fade. The play hopes to exploit the one-on-one matchup between a wide receiver and cornerback near the goal line. Taking the snap under center, the quarterback lofts a jump ball for the wideout to fetch in the back corner of the end zone. It is a play that takes skill and unending practice due to the timing needed between thrower and catcher.

If the play was called for Mike Evans, one would have little reason to argue. But the call was made for Manziel to try the fade with freshman receiver Ja'Quay Williams, a player with just one career reception on passes from Manziel.

As it was familiar, Manziel lobbed a soft pass to the back corner and watched it fall into the hands of Alabama defensive back Cyrus Jones for a punishing interception. Instead of following the path of the pass, Williams, the receiver, stopped after four strides and attempted to post up Jones like an NBA center. As the ball flew over Williams' head, Jones released and made a terrific play on the ball. Taking over at the A&M 20, McCarron completed two passes, the final one, a 51 yard touchdown throw, allowed Alabama to take their first lead of the football game.

Alabama's turnovers in 2012 were at the heart of the previous year's shocking A&M victory. McCarron threw two interceptions in the upset including a game clinching pick at the A&M goal line late in the fourth quarter. Turnovers would bear an even bigger role in the rematch with no single play being more crucial than Manziel's errant throw as the third quarter opened.

Manziel began his first drive of the second half with a nine yard rush to the A&M 43. The Aggies, trailing 28-14 after a late first half touchdown by Alabama, began the half with a solid hold of the Crimson Tide offense. Forcing the Alabama punt had brought the 12th Man back into the game. Under a roar, Manziel hurried the offense to the line, received a quick snap and tried to get all fourteen points back in one throw.

The target on Manziel's pass was senior Travis Labhart. Running a seam route up the right third of the field, Labhart was blanketed by an over-the-top safety and underneath linebacker. The A&M quarterback forced a bullet to the wideout striking the nearest Alabama defender in the helmet, sending the football end over end and high into the air.

Resting beneath the falling deflection was Alabama safety Vinnie Sunseri. He cradled the interception and ran. With a wall of Crimson Tide teammates providing safe passage, Sunseri rumbled 73 yards for a touchdown. 90 seconds into half two, A&M was behind 35-14.

McKinney took the ball out of Manziel's hands on A&M's next drive. A strange notion to consider undoubtedly, but the decision allowed the effective A&M offensive line to flex their considerable muscle and soothe the rattled nerves of the Aggies.

Running backs Malena and Tra Carson traded carries moving the football from the A&M 42 to the Tide 14 yard line. At this junction, Manziel's number was called. The quarterback responded by whipping a pass over the middle to wideout Malcome Kennedy for a touchdown. The scoring drive removed three minutes from the clock and A&M had closed the gap to 35-21.

The remainder of the third quarter and the opening 90 seconds of the fourth was a trade of punts and touchdowns. Kenyan Drake's three yard touchdown run for Alabama was matched by Kennedy's second touchdown catch early in the fourth. Drives between saw mammoth 60 yard punts from the Tide's Cody Mandell and the Aggies' Drew Kaser.

The score read Alabama 42, Texas A&M 28. The time remaining was 13 minutes and 20 seconds. If A&M was to close the gap and make the game a legitimate contest, the Aggie defense and offense would have to make big plays in unison. A proposal that had little faith attached as the Crimson Tide was again plowing through the Aggies' front defensive seven on their way to a potential game securing score. Their backs against the goal line, the A&M defense made an unlikely stand highlighted by an unbelievable play.

Manziel now had the ball at the four yard line.

A revitalized 12th Man looked to their savior.

When their savior needed a miracle he turned to Mike Evans.

Standing six feet and five inches tall, with long muscular arms adorned with multi-colored tattoos, Mike Evans certainly is an imposing figure.

Born to a teenage mother, Evans grew up in a tough part of Galveston fraught with environmental hazards such as drug dealing and violent crime. There are several realities Mike could have lived but early in his life his mother, Heather Kilgore, decided those dangerous avenues would not swallow her son.

Keeping Evans and his sister involved in sports was her primary tool. "I always tried to put them in stuff and keep them busy," Kilgore told Joshua Siegel of the *Eagle*. "I didn't want them to go the wrong way. He was always in a tournament or going somewhere."

That "somewhere" usually involved basketball, Evans' first love. Refusing to play football despite constant hounding from the football coaches at Galveston Ball High School, Evans had his heart set on a career playing basketball for the University of Texas. The problem was Longhorns' basketball coach Rick Barnes, and his staff in Austin, didn't think much of Evans. "They didn't seem interested in him, so he wasn't interested in them," said Kilgore.

Seeing that his dream to play for the Longhorns was on shaky ground, Evans opened himself up to the possibility of playing football. "We bugged him all the time," said Ball head football coach David Suggs. "If it wasn't me, it was my defensive coordinator, and if it wasn't him, it was the offensive coordinator. He was getting double-and triple teamed to give him more opportunities to come out and offer him a chance to play at the collegiate level."

Evans decided to give it a shot. The choice yielded immediate results. "The first day we put on pads (in high school)," Evans said. "I got a (scholarship) offer from Tulane."

His lone season of football impressed Mike Sherman's A&M staff who loved Evans' athleticism and versatility. During an unofficial visit to College Station, the future wide receiver was convinced and committed to A&M.

Soon after his decision, Barnes and the Longhorns came calling, flipping their earlier feelings about Evans' potential as a basketball player. Mike turned down their offer, packed his bags and headed to Aggieland.

Significant confusion as to what position Evans should play forced the A&M coaching staff to redshirt the wide receiver. There was the belief by some coaches that Evans' size was perfect for a tight end, and the year off would allow Mike to add heft to his frame. But soon into his practice sessions with scout team quarterback Johnny Manziel, everyone knew Evans' skills were too special to play anything but wide receiver.

The newly minted wideout spent the remainder of his redshirt year becoming complete with endless drills to improve footwork and explosion off the line. Players like Evans become known when they are given opportunities in huge games. There would be no bigger stage than the SEC and the wide receiver was ready to step into the spotlight.

Alabama began the drive, moments after Kennedy made his second touchdown catch, on their own 25 yard line. The crowd, loud and begging for a stop from the young A&M defense, was silenced in one play as McCarron connected with White on a 26 yard reception. In just one play the Tide were in A&M territory. From there the dynamic running back from Alabama, T.J. Yeldon was handed the ball seven straight times. The first six carries went for 33 yards, with a debilitating 15 yard personal foul against the Aggies mixed in, placing the ball on A&M's one yard line.

Needing three feet to put the Tide back up by 21, the call was made for Yeldon's seventh consecutive carry. McCarron received the snap cleanly and turned to give the ball to Yeldon. The running back took the handoff low to the ground hoping to bruise his way over the goal line.

Shooting the gap Yeldon was to run through was Aggies' free safety, the 200 pound, Clay Honeycutt. As low as Yeldon was, Honeycutt seemed to be lower, charging into the running back and exploding upward. The collision sent Yeldon vertical and shot the ball from his hands. A&M fell upon the fumble. Evans and Manziel burst from the sideline.

Backed into their own end zone, the Aggies failed to move the ball on first and second down. Facing a long third down and nine, McKinney called for a formation with two receivers to Manziel's left and a lone receiver, Evans, posted far to the right. The first two passing options on the play were to the wideouts on the left. McKinney wasn't looking to go deep; he just wanted a first down to prolong the drive.

Evans was the final option on the play. He was to run up the field for fifteen yards then break out toward the sideline and back up the field again.

Manziel took the shotgun snap and dropped back into an end zone covered in late afternoon shadows. He looked left. Both receivers to that side were draped by Alabama. Flashing his eyes right, he saw Evans streaking ahead of the Tide cornerback. He threw the pass like a javelin, with his back foot coming forward and his body twisting.

Evans ran to the ball. He had a lead on the Tide cornerback, slight as it was, and extended his hands to meet the pass. Popping up in his hands, Evans was able to secure the ball.

A footrace commenced. Cyrus Jones, the Alabama cornerback on the wide receiver's heels, gained ground because Evans was beginning to cramp. With rope-tight legs, the wideout turned and stuck an arm in Jones' facemask. The defender stunned by the contact, lost the rhythm of his gait and slowed. Evans glided into the end zone 95 yards from where the play began.

In a day with numerous eruptions from the 12th Man, there was no louder outburst than the one following Evans as he ran for the touchdown. Manziel, manic in his gestures as he trailed Evans, pointed to the sky, the crowd, and his teammates. He was a roaring firework with buzzing Roman candle legs.

The awe-invoking celebration provided the day's greatest high for Manziel, Evans, and the rest of the Aggies. The seven point deficit was as close as A&M would come to victory.

Saban stumbled onto the field to shake Sumlin's hand looking like a punchdrunk boxer. He knew his team was fortunate to leave Kyle Field with a 49-42 win over the Aggies. "We knew we were going to have to play this way on offense to have a chance in this game," Saban said. "I didn't think they were going to score 42 points, but I kind of thought they would score some points and they did."

The efforts of Manziel and Evans, throughout the battle versus the Crimson Tide, were astonishing. The wide receiver made seven catches for 279 yards, smashing the A&M single game record for receiving yardage. Manziel threw for a career best 464 yards, adding 98 more via the ground and five touchdown passes. The 628 yards of total offense A&M gained against the Crimson Tide were the most ever surrendered by a Saban-coached Alabama team.

Discussion after the game did not focus on the Tide's win but rather the reinforcement of Johnny Manziel as college football's best player. "He plays the game in a way we've rarely seen, and he seems to enjoy it as much as we hope we would," said Andy Staples of Sports Illustrated. "There's a reason he won the Heisman," Alabama safety Vinnie Sunseri said. "He's an unbelievable player, I don't care what he does off the field."

Accolades aside, Manziel was frustrated after the loss. His two interceptions, leading to 14 Tide points, was the difference in a game where the A&M defense provided no margin for error. The quarterback shouldered those mistaken throws after the game, saying the turnovers were "on me." But his face tightened when writers asked if A&M's season was over. "This wasn't the Super Bowl," Manziel said. "Alabama lost a game last year and still went on to win the national championship. Our season isn't over."

6 SMU & Arkansas

"**I** have the worst job in America this week," said Southern Methodist University defensive coordinator Tom Mason. His task, deciding how to defend against Johnny Manziel, was harsh, cruel work that had no easy answers. "He creates so much stuff with his feet, with his scrambling ability," Mason said. "He's got a real uncanny ability to throw the ball as he scrambles. He's going to get some on you. You have to try to minimize it by creating a turnover here or there. I think the worst thing you can do is change your structure. You do what you do and see what happens."

Manziel, a week removed from his 562 yard performance versus an Alabama defense many considered to be the stingiest in the country, had become impossible to game plan against. "I don't think you stop him," Oklahoma defensive coordinator Mike Stoops said after the Cotton Bowl. "Nobody has been able to stop him. I think you try to contain him and try to limit his big plays. Being able to keep him in the pocket is easier said than done…His ability to extend and create plays, there's not a defense created to defend against that."

The two teams from the 2012 season that did create a defense to hold Manziel in check, LSU and Florida, had the benefit of being strong, athletic defenses full of five star recruits. SMU did not have a defense anyone would characterize as strong or athletic. Through their first two games, against Texas Tech and Montana State, the Mustangs had been lit up for 35.5 points per game, 315 yards through the air, and allowed teams to convert third downs almost 50% of the time. The chances of keeping Manziel under control looked utterly beyond reason. Regardless, the 28 point underdogs were like most teams, eager to play the reigning Heisman winner. "We're going in there with the attitude that we've got to take the ball away and keep Johnny Football on the sideline," senior SMU cornerback Kenneth Acker said. "You've got to go in there knowing that at any point he could go off on one of those ad-lib moments. You can't go off of what you see on film. You've got to play the play instead of the scheme."

If there was a worry in College Station it centered around the fear the Alabama game had drained the Aggies and left them with little enthusiasm for their week four game against the Mustangs. Compounding the issue was the existential question introduced after the Alabama loss – *who were these Aggies?* Before the Crimson Tide battle, ESPN analyst David Pollack asked, "What are (the Aggies) going to do this year? One year doesn't qualify as a rise. Nick Saban took Alabama and put them on the rise pretty quickly. Urban Meyer took Florida on the rise, but

86

they won championships in their second year there. So I think that story's unwritten, but it was a heck of a first year. I don't think anybody saw that coming. It's great and it's going in that direction, but you got to tell me what happens this year before I start putting them into categories."

What happened in the few days leading up to the contest with SMU was a defiant assurance that the Aggies' spirit was not broken. "I don't think it'll be difficult at all for us as a team (to be ready)," senior running back Ben Malena said. "That's what champions do, they play at a consistent level and have similar emotions on a week-to-week basis. We do understand last week was a big game, and it's going to be challenging to have that same kind of enthusiasm just because of the circumstances, but our play on the field is not going to change. We're still going to be the same team we were last week this week."

After SMU's opening drive ended with a punt to midfield, the collective worry of the 86,542 in attendance at Kyle Field disappeared on A&M's first offensive play. Manziel connected with sophomore wideout Sabian Holmes on a 33 yard pass and catch, moving the football inside the Mustangs' 20 yard line. A 12 yard draw by Manziel put the Aggies on the doorstep, then Malena crossed the threshold to give the Aggies an early 7-0 lead. The one minute, fifty second drive spanned 52 yards in five plays.

The Aggie offense scored their second touchdown after the A&M defense forced their second consecutive punt. Beginning at their own 20, Manziel and Malena took turns gutting the SMU defense. The pair had five rushes for 39 yards on the drive, with Manziel mixing in a 46 yard bomb to Mike Evans. The quarterback capped the drive with a seven yard touchdown run and extended the A&M lead to fourteen.

A surprise onside kick kept the Aggie offense on the field but the drive pulled up lame when Manziel's pass into the end zone was intercepted by SMU free safety Hayden Greenbauer. It was Manziel's second red zone turnover in as many weeks. The Mustangs drove the ball into A&M territory before stalling and settling for a 42 yard field goal from Chase Hover. The first quarter ended with the Mustangs looking at an eleven point deficit.

There was a noticeable relaxation at Kyle Field. The sold out crowd appeared to be disinterested, the extent of their applause and fervor nowhere near the level it was the week before. Same could be said for the A&M offense. Manziel had only eight pass attempts against the team's 13 rushes. The run first, run often strategy continued on A&M's fifth offensive drive of the game. Malena was given the ball on the first four plays and after six of seven run calls, McKinney gave Manziel the signal to bring the drive home. Facing a third and two, Manziel connected with Malcome Kennedy on a 16 yard touchdown. The extra point was missed and the lead was seventeen at 20-3.

Kennedy caught two more passes on the next drive, totaling 41 yards, setting up two Manziel rushes. The final run, from seven yards, put the Aggie quarterback into the end zone for a second time. The extra point was unsuccessful again and the A&M lead was extended to 26-3.

In an embarrassment of riches, the Aggie defense scored on the first play of the following drive. SMU's quarterback, Garrett Gilbert, connected with freshman wideout Jeremiah Gaines on a short pass over the middle. Gaines was then hit by Toney Hurd Jr., the Aggies senior cornerback and the ball came loose. The fumble was scooped up by fellow cornerback Deshazor Everett and the junior walked into the end zone from 12 yards. In just over three minutes the Aggies had scored three touchdowns. The extra attempt was not missed this time. It was blocked. The scoreboard read Aggies 32, Mustangs 3. SMU would add another field goal as the clock expired and the first half ended 32-6 in A&M's favor.

A&M received the opening second half kickoff. Manziel's last drive of the game encompassed eight plays - seven rushes and one pass. The quarterback was responsible for 59 yards of the drive before handing the ball to Malena and watching the senior score his second touchdown of the day. Sumlin told Manziel to grab a towel and his visor. With a 39-6 lead, his day was done.

Even though there was a collective yawn in College Station at Manziel's 346 yards and three touchdowns against the Mustangs, the same apathy did not infect whoever the Aggies' weekly opponent may be. Every week a fresh set of young men worked themselves into a lather of anticipation facing college football's most visible personality. For their fifth game of 2013, the ninth ranked Aggies were to travel to Little Rock, Arkansas to take on their second SEC opponent of the year, the Arkansas Razorbacks. The Hogs blew a 17 point lead the week before against Rutgers, a frustrating loss that had the Razorback defense looking for retribution. For their pain, they could not imagine a better outlet than the body of Manziel. "Everybody wants a piece of him," said Arkansas defensive end Chris Smith.

Although the Razorbacks had bloodlust in their eyes, the Arkansas coaches had trepidation in their approach to defending Manziel. One of the first matters new Arkansas head coach Bret Bielema undertook after accepting the position was to spend two full days watching A&M game film from 2012. "(Manziel's) a guy who just has an uncanny way to deliver the ball, no matter where he's at on the field," Bielema said. "Some of those plays he's stayed alive on are from anywhere from a slow count of six seconds to 10-12 seconds. I like confident people and Johnny Manziel is a very confident person. I think that's fun to observe and watch. And hopefully, that swagger has a little effect on our guys."

Hoping to carry the swagger to Little Rock was the A&M defense after their stellar performance against SMU. The challenge for the Aggies would lie in their ability to stop the run, something they failed to do against Alabama. Under Bielema, the Razorbacks were a power running team, gaining close to 1,000 rushing yards in their first four games. Arkansas needed to run the ball well to keep the clock moving and Manziel off the field.

The problem for Arkansas, at the beginning of the game, was they had no choice but to give the ball to Manziel. The Aggies, winners of the coin toss, had chosen to receive. After the Razorbacks' kicker Zach Hocker put the football through the back of the end zone, Manziel stood at the Aggies' 25 yard line awaiting the snap. A&M ran the ball 48 times against SMU, with eight coming on first downs. Sensing an opportunity, A&M offensive coordinator Clarence McKinney called for a play action pass. Manziel took the snap and faked a handoff to Ben Malena. Streaking down the field was wideout Mike Evans on a deep post route. Manziel threw a gorgeous pass hitting Evans for 49 yards. In one play the Aggies were at Arkansas' 26 yard line. Completions to Malena and Malcome Kennedy put the Aggies inside the Razorbacks' ten yard line. On third and four, Arkansas only rushed four defenders dropping back seven into coverage. Manziel, with all the time in the world, floated to his right and sent a missile into the back corner of the end zone that was caught by Evans. The touchdown capped a six play, 75 yard drive taking two minutes and thirty nine seconds off the clock. A&M had now scored first 17 of 18 times under Sumlin.

The Razorbacks were equally as good on their first drive. With a healthy Brandon Allen under center, the quarterback, who missed the game against Rutgers with a bum shoulder, used the air to strike for two huge third down conversions. The first, a 29 yard completion to Javontee Herndon, moved the football into A&M territory. The second, a play action pass that froze Aggie safety Howard Matthews, put the Razorbacks on the scoreboard as Allen found Keon Hatcher in the end zone to tie the game at seven.

Rhythm established on the first A&M drive carried over to the second charge as Manziel completed three passes over the first five plays. Two catches by Kennedy and another by Evans moved the football to the Arkansas 41 yard line. Facing a third and ten, Manziel dropped back to throw and watched as the center of the football field became empty. The resulting 20 yard scramble moved the chains to the Razorbacks' 21. From there Tra Carson, a sledge hammer running back that transferred to A&M from Oregon, plowed his way to the Arkansas two yard line. The nineteen yard run by the six foot, 250 pound sophomore set up Malena's two yard touchdown one play later. Two drives, two touchdowns and the Aggies lead was back to seven.

After an Arkansas punt, the Aggies and Razorbacks traded field goals. On A&M's first drive of the second quarter, McKinney decided to grind the Arkansas front seven defenders into dust. Seven of the first eight plays were rushes. Manziel had 27 yards on the ground to accompany Malena's 15 and Brandon Williams' 18 yards on the drive. On third and six, from the Arkansas seven yard line, Manziel took the shotgun snap and was surrounded by blitzing defenders. He scrambled and lobbed a pass in the direction of the tall, athletic Evans. The receiver from Galveston leapt up and reached over two Arkansas defensive backs, ripping the ball out of the air and landing with his feet in the end zone. The jump ball touchdown gave the Aggies their biggest lead of the night at 24-10.

With the exception of the second A&M touchdown, Arkansas had responded to every Aggie scoring drive with one of their own. Their fourth offensive drive of the game was no different as Allen marched the Razorbacks offense 82 yards, connecting with Jonathan Williams for his second touchdown pass of the game. Later, after A&M was finally forced to punt, the Razorbacks added a field goal before halftime and the teams went to their locker rooms with the score standing at A&M 24, Arkansas 20.

The second half opened with the A&M defense getting their second touchdown in as many weeks. Safety Deshazor Everett came between an Allen pass and his intended target, intercepted the football, and returned it 34 yards for a touchdown. The game of - can you top this - continued on Arkansas' next drive as the Razorbacks marched the length of the field in four plays and the A&M lead was back to a mere four.

With rain now covering the artificial surface of Razorback stadium, McKinney decided to rely less on his quarterback and more on his hulking offensive line in the second half. Manziel took the field and assumed his new role of handoff master. In the third quarter, the Aggies would run 18 offensive plays. 15 of those were runs. Minutes after trading touchdowns, the two teams swapped punts. A&M started their second offensive drive of the second half at their own 32 yard line. The nine play, all rush drive was capped with Trey Williams' 17 yard rush for a touchdown. The lead was back to eleven, 38-27. Then it wasn't. Arkansas ended the third quarter with their own touchdown drive. The two point conversion failed and the score as the fourth quarter began stood at 38-33.

Both offenses failed to move the football early in the fourth quarter. After an A&M punt, the Razorbacks went three-and-out giving Manziel terrific field position at the A&M 43 yard line. McKinney called seven straight runs. Carson and Trey Williams did the heavy lifting combining on five rushes that moved the ball just short of the Arkansas goal line. From one yard, Malena crossed the goal line for his second touchdown. The twelve point cushion would not be relinquished.

Arkansas had two chances to get back into the game and the A&M defense forced turnovers on both possessions. Once on downs, the other a Steven Jenkins interception that iced the game. Manziel put the knee down, watched the clock run out and jogged off the field. The final score read Texas A&M 45, Arkansas 33.

As he was in the second half, Manziel remained quiet after the game. He continued to be perfect on the road as the Aggie quarterback was now 9-0 when traveling in his collegiate career. The confidence lost after the defeat to Alabama was slowly restoring itself. It was a necessary thing as the Aggies were about to head into a crucial section of their season with games against Mississippi State, Auburn, and their next opponent, Ole Miss. The A&M football team would have two weeks to get ready for their trip to Oxford. They would need the down time because they were in store for a slugfest.

7 Ole Miss

Ole Miss starting quarterback Bo Wallace had seen the ease in which Alabama and Arkansas had scored against the young, vulnerable Texas A&M defense. He knew his Rebels' offense, averaging 27 points per game, could and probably *would* be successful against the Aggies. So with his team exhausted after playing four of their first five games on the road and reeling after back to back losses against Alabama and Auburn, Wallace stepped up to the microphone at Ole Miss's weekly press conference foaming at the mouth. Adhering to the steadfast sports principle that leadership does not have to be faithful to the truth, Wallace declared his Ole Miss offense "could score on anyone." The tall, blond junior quarterback was either indifferent or openly ignoring the fact that Alabama had held the Rebels scoreless two weeks ago.

Despite the leap in logic, Wallace decided Ole Miss needed to hear a fearless, acidic voice to aid in stopping their recent stumble. After pumping up the qualities of his offense, he began to pump shots at Texas A&M. On the heels of divulging that he had encouraged his teammates to "just be nasty" with the Aggies, Wallace took aim at those who catch Johnny

Manziel's passes. "I think we have better receivers than A&M," Wallace said. The media, always on the lookout for the central thread to fill their columns in the empty days leading to a game, were more than pleased when Wallace hand delivered a meaty topic to discuss and gently placed it in their laps.

As writers are known to do, they hurried to the A&M coaching staff and shoved Wallace's comments directly in the ears of A&M's offensive coordinator Clarence McKinney. "I don't want to get into that," McKinney said. "I like the guys we have." It wasn't hard to see the grin that accompanied McKinney's words.

If Wallace was trying to shoehorn the narrative that his receivers were more talented than Manziel's, he would need something other than facts to prove his opinion. The A&M offense was ranked in the top seven in the nation in several categories that relied heavily upon the quality of their receiving corps. The Aggies were near the top in passing offense, total offense, scoring offense, passing efficiency and third down efficiency. In those select categories the best Mississippi could muster was a 52nd place in the total offense, the rest were far worse.

What Wallace could not fathom was the depth A&M held at the wide receiver position. Through the first five games, Aggie quarterbacks had completed passes to seventeen different players. It was a deeply skilled group Manziel had the luxury of throwing to each week. Many, despite being low on the depth chart, had the potential to breakout and take over a game if the opportunity to do so arose. Early in the Ole Miss game, when the Rebels' defense made a strategic choice, Wallace would soon discover his well-intentioned belief had been hijacked and refuted by a small, unknown A&M wideout who had long been working on a narrative of his own.

Travis Labhart arrived on the Texas A&M campus in the fall of 2009 with no intention or desire to play football. His mind was focused on making the Aggies' men basketball team as a walk on. A talented shooter out of Whitesboro, Texas, Labhart believed he had the skills necessary to be a player useful to the Aggies' 2009-2010 team. The coaches disagreed. Labhart, rejected on his first attempt, wanted to stay in basketball shape so he accepted an invitation to join the all-male practice squad for the Lady Aggies' basketball team. Everyday Labhart battled against a women's team that would soon win a national championship. There was nothing on the line for Labhart within these workouts but he was praised by the Lady Aggies' staff for his tireless ability to play with energy.

On the eve of the 2010-11 basketball season, Labhart tried once more to make the men's team. The result was identical to his previous attempt. Cited for his lack of size (Labhart stands at 5 feet 9 inches and at the time weighed less than 180 pounds) the coaches informed Travis his dream of playing college basketball would likely not happen at A&M. For the first time in his athletic career Labhart was left with doubt, a feeling that had him spinning and without direction. "You worked so hard for something and you don't attain it – it's really difficult," Labhart said. "I remember going home that fall when I didn't make the team just crushed."

Labhart went away with his family for Christmas break. In the mountains of Colorado he cleared his head, watched A&M play LSU in the Cotton Bowl, and came to a peculiar decision about his future.

He wanted to play football.

Once the mind was focused, the body followed. Labhart went to work immediately filling his days with weights, sprints, and endless games of catch with his brother. Football wasn't completely foreign to Labhart as he had played quarterback and safety in high school but that was over three years ago. To perform at the level A&M demanded, Labhart would have to do more than obsessively train. He would have to become accustomed to ignoring the word "no."

Three months later Labhart was in pads when A&M opened their spring camp. With impressive speed and athleticism, the Aggies' coaching staff invited Labhart to continue his pursuit for a walk-on role in the fall. He had not made the team but if he improved over the summer, chances were good Labhart would become a member of the 2011 team.

Come fall Labhart's inexperience undermined his chances and he was once again cut by an Aggies' men sports team. This rejection, however, had a silver lining. The Aggie staff was blunt with Labhart. He would not find his way onto the 105 man traveling squad but they wanted him to work as a receiver on the scout team.

This is where he met Johnny Manziel.

Manziel, recently redshirted, was installed as the scout team quarterback. In addition to the practices, the scout team was prepped to mimic the coming week's opponent. This required long, dull film sessions from Labhart and Manziel, and the pair became fast friends. They both decided they would use these practices to showcase their abilities to the coaching staff, embarrass the starters, and, most of all, encourage one another to have a damned good time. Through thousands of Manziel passes and thousands of Labhart catches a connection was born.

The following season as Manziel's career flourished, Labhart's stalled. Slowed by nagging injuries to his foot and abdomen, Labhart lost his entire 2012 season. In the offseason, before his last year of eligibility, Labhart became dedicated to creating a body that would last. He entered the 2013 spring workouts in the best shape of his life only to watch his fleeting dream take another shot when he broke his collarbone on one of the last days of camp.

What endears the coaching staff to a player and a project such as Labhart is his inability to quit. He is what coaches refer to as a grinder, the type of player who is first to practice and last to leave. Labhart, like Manziel, craved more – more knowledge, more repetitions of a route, as he never grew tired of the monotony of run and catch. This is what enabled the relationship with Manziel to blossom. The confidence Johnny had in Travis had grown to lengths the A&M offense coaching staff could no longer ignore. Keeping Labhart off the field was denying Manziel another weapon and by extension, denying the team additional points. Before the Ole Miss game, the receiver was told to be ready for more, much more, as his role in the offense would be expanding.

A&M received the opening kickoff in the end zone and the return man, Trey Williams, brought it out to the Aggies' 22 yard line. Manziel took the opening snap and bounced on his toes, looking for a receiver. With nothing to his liking, Manziel, never one for patience, left the comfort of the pocket and ran for 17 yards. The play itself was quintessential Manziel, sliding agility accompanied by bursts of electric speed but it also held the crucial information A&M's staff was looking for. Since the Alabama game, Mike Evans was seeing a healthy dose of double teams. This was an attempt, by defensive coordinators, to prevent Evans' freakish ability from completely taking over a game. By doing this, the door became open for A&M wideouts, such as Labhart, to expect one-on-one coverage from the opponent's lesser defensive backs. Sure enough, as Evans left the line on the first play, two Ole Miss defensive backs sandwiched the talented wideout. The stage was now set for another A&M receiver to potentially have a huge game.

After a nine yard scramble by Manziel moved the chains, and the ball, into Ole Miss territory, Labhart made the biggest catch of his young career. Entering the game, Labhart had only three catches and 52 yards for the 2013 season. But facing a third down and seven to go, Manziel targeted Labhart. The wideout made a crucial 35 yard catch advancing the ball inside the Rebels' ten yard line. Ben Malena scored on a seven yard run, one play later, to give A&M an early 7-0 lead. Manziel found a beaming Labhart on the sideline and told the wide receiver there was no going back as he had finally made the big time. Looking around the sold out Vaught-Hemingway Stadium Labhart certainly hoped what Manziel was telling him would remain true.

Penalties and incompletions spoiled the Rebels' first drive as they gave the ball back to the Aggies after a failed fourth down attempt. The bizarre call by head coach Hugh Freeze gave A&M the ball on the Ole Miss' 45 yard line. After moving quickly to the Rebels' 24 yard line, Manziel took the first down exchange from center and rolled to his left. As he planted to throw he became ensnared in the artificial field turf surface. The left knee of the quarterback buckled and Manziel fell to the turf reaching for the source of his pain. Silence rippled through the several thousand Aggie fans that made the drive to Oxford, Mississippi as their quarterback rolled in anguish beneath them. Trainers rushed to Manziel's side and slowly put him through strength tests to determine the severity of the damage. Following a few tense minutes, Manziel nodded and was helped to his feet. Under applause from the Ole Miss crowd, that perhaps lacked sincerity, the quarterback was guided to a bench on the A&M sideline. Without Manziel, the Aggies' drive stalled. As Josh Lambo missed a 36 yard field goal, the quarterback was fitted for a knee brace. Gingerly he began to throw on the sideline and test the mobility of his ailing knee. Manziel responded well and word was sent to Sumlin. His quarterback was ready to return.

As Manziel was working out the kinks, sophomore cornerback De'Vante Harris was blowing his assignment. Unsure if he was to defend Ole Miss wideout Vince Sanders in man or zone, Harris allowed the speedy receiver to slide behind him. Wallace hit Sanders and seventy yards later the game was tied.

60,000 pairs of eyes gawked at Manziel's tender left knee as the quarterback returned to the field. Gingerly, he completed his first three passes moving the football from his own 25 yard line to the Rebels' 35. After a personal foul on Ole Miss, Manziel gave the ball to Williams and the running back found the end zone from eighteen yards. The five play, 75 yard drive took less than two minutes off the clock and soothed a frazzled A&M sideline as Manziel showed no signs of lingering pain. Before halftime Ole Miss added a late field goal and the Aggies entered the locker room with a 14-10 advantage.

In the previous year's game Ole Miss had success by leaving a roaming defender to shadow Manziel. The offensive coaches at A&M, anticipating the Rebels would use a similar scheme this year, spent the week implementing several plays out of a five receiver, empty backfield set. The theory, that spreading the field would allow Manziel more room to roam, was proven by the 71 yards the signal caller rushed for in the first half.

The Aggies' defense, displaying a growing toughness, opened the second half by forcing the third Ole Miss punt. Manziel, utilizing the mismatches provided by the extra wideout formation, used both arm and legs to create A&M's third touchdown drive of the game. The A&M signal caller was perfect on the opening drive of the second half completing all four passes including two to Labhart. Manziel's five yard rush and dive into the end zone pushed the Aggies' lead to eleven.

Coach Freeze used both his starter and backup quarterback, Barry Brunetti, on the following drive. After Wallace led the Rebels to consecutive first downs, Brunetti assumed the helm and guided the offense to their second touchdown of the game. The backup quarterback's 16 yard hookup with freshman wideout Laquon Treadwell shrunk the A&M lead to four at 21-17.

With the A&M offense in a yard-chewing groove, Labhart would have his best drive of the game. His four catches for 36 yards was all for naught, however, when Manziel attempted to thread a pass through three Ole Miss defenders. The resulting interception would be regifted three plays later by the unsteady Wallace. A&M linebacker Darian

Clairborne's pickoff allowed Josh Lambo to tack on a 37 yard field goal as the fourth quarter began. The A&M lead was back to seven.

The fourth quarter was nothing short of an exasperating track meet. After the Lambo field goal, Ole Miss raced down the field and tied the game in less than three minutes. On A&M's next possession, Manziel fumbled the ball away to Ole Miss. The Rebels' offense took advantage when Wallace settled and connected with Treadwell on the talented young receiver's second touchdown of the game. In 76 seconds, a seven point deficit had become a seven point lead for the Rebels.

Trey Williams returned the following kickoff to the A&M 25 yard line. Mississippi stuffed a first down Manziel run attempt then pressured the quarterback into an incompletion on down two. The crowd at Vaught-Hemingway Stadium was roaring as Manziel brought the Aggie offense to the line facing a third and nine. The quarterback took the exchange and snapped a throw to Derel Walker on the left sideline. Shy of the first down, Walker spun out of a tackle and broke into the open field for a gain of 27 yards. Manziel then found Malcome Kennedy twice to put A&M inside Ole Miss's ten yard line. Williams finished the drive on the following play by scoring on a nine yard run. The touchdown drive covered seventy-five yards in less than two minutes and thirty seconds. The scoreboard standing above the silent, gut-punched Mississippi crowd read 31-31.

The strong first half defense by A&M was not replicated in the second. The third and fourth quarter was littered with penalties, dropped interceptions, and badly missed assignments. None worse than when Ole Miss running back Jayton Walton floated out the backfield without anyone from the A&M defense taking note. Wallace dropped a pass into Walton's hands and the sophomore waltzed 50 yards down the sideline to give Ole Miss a seven point advantage. Manziel watched Walton cross the goal line on the video board. He turned to Labhart, sitting near an adjacent bench, and grinned while shaking his head.

There was six minutes left in the game when the A&M offense returned to the field. Trailing by seven, Manziel jump started the drive with consecutive completions to Evans and Kennedy, moving the ball into Mississippi territory. The Ole Miss defense stiffened and forced the Aggies into a fourth and seven. Coach Sumlin motioned for the offense to stay on the field. On the crucial fourth down A&M's quarterback took the shotgun snap and stood in the pocket. The Rebels' pass rush had slowly run out of gas due to the up tempo, no huddle A&M offense, and they were nonexistent during Manziel's time in the pocket. The play had time to develop and the receivers had the rare opportunity to finish their routes. With the Ole Miss secondary stretched from sideline to sideline, the center of the field became a ghost town. Manziel checked his receivers one last time, then with the football away from his body, ran to the vacancy. A step after gaining the first down, Manziel was hit as he tried to tuck the football. The ball was knocked loose and into Manziel's stomach, a lucky break giving the quarterback an opportunity to gain control as he fell to the surface. Johnny popped up and signaled for his team to get in position, there was no celebration from the quarterback but the Aggie alumni and fans were frantic with excitement.

The hair-raising fourth down pickup was followed by Mike Evans' biggest play of the game. The wideout, tempered by the game long double team, caught a Manziel throw and gained 26 yards giving the Aggies another first and goal at the Mississippi eight yard line.

Nearing three minutes to go, Manziel took the shotgun snap and drifted to the right side of the pocket. The Ole Miss left end, freshman Robert Nkemdiche, slid around the tackle and pushed Manziel to his left. With the pocket collapsing and everyone shadowing Manziel, the left side of the field had become open. The quarterback evaded the pressure and fled to the left goal line pylon. As Manziel neared the end zone he dove and extended the football, clipping the soft electric-orange marker. The official raised his hands and the game was tied at 38.

With Manziel's touchdown, Ole Miss quarterback Bo Wallace would be given a chance to back up the proclamations he made during the week. But instead of leading a possible game winning drive, Wallace threw three straight incompletions forcing the Rebels to punt. By missing an open check down to his running back on third down, Wallace committed the unforgivable sin of allowing Manziel back onto the football field.

The final drive of the football game began at the Aggies' 29 yard line. On the first down, with the game clock at 2:33, Manziel found Kennedy on a fourteen yard completion. The Ole Miss defense, who had already been torched by the A&M offense for more than 500 yards, surrendered 25 more on back-to-back Manziel rushes. As the clock continued its descent toward zero, A&M running backs pushed the football through the weary Rebels' defense to the fifteen yard line of Ole Miss. With four seconds left, Sumlin signaled for timeout. Lambo walked onto the field to prepare for the possible game winning field goal.

Manziel walked to the sideline and removed his helmet. Met by several teammates, the group formed a circle. As they prayed on bended knee, Lambo stepped off the kick and with a good snap and hold, he drove the football inside the right upright.

The Texas A&M sideline exploded and ran onto the field. Not witnessing the kick that won the game did not mean Manziel was late to the celebration. Once the sideline roared, Manziel burst from his kneel and joined the rush to greet Lambo. The kicker, who doubled as a member of the A&M soccer team, broke free from his teammates on the field and ran toward the oncoming rush of the sideline. He dropped to his knees and slid, his arms raised, screaming to the sky. He was swallowed in an abyss of celebration.

The final quarter saw two fourth down conversions, no offensive drive lasting longer than three minutes, 386 total yards, six lead changes and a total of 41 points scored between the two teams. It was a flawed, gasping, and ultimately thrilling final fifteen minutes of football.

After the game reporters surrounded Labhart. His final line of eight catches and 97 yards led the *Eagle's* Robert Cessna to quip that the fifth year senior "didn't just have a career day – he had a career." Although Labhart did not find the end zone he was instrumental on two important touchdown drives. "This time of the year if you're going to win, you're going to have to have guys (like Labhart) play at a high level that weren't talked about before the season," Sumlin said. Instead of singing his own praises Labhart spent his moment in front of the microphones heaping praise upon the individual who threw him the football. "I've never been around such a gamer," Labhart said. "We were confident. I never doubted."

Following the fumble that allowed Ole Miss to take the lead early in the fourth quarter, Manziel completed six of eight passes for 118 yards and posted 45 yards and a touchdown on five carries. "Johnny's a beast. Week in - week out, we can expect greatness from him," Lambo said.

"The beast" walked slowly off the field. The knee was sore and the rest of him beaten from the hits taken in his season-high nineteen carries. Yet Manziel smiled and sang fight songs alongside his teammates. He was exhausted and proud and headed back to

109

College Station to ready himself for a primetime Saturday afternoon matchup against college football's most surprising team.

8 Auburn

Riding the lone season of Heisman Trophy winning and future Carolina Panthers quarterback Cam Newton, the 2010 Auburn Tigers bested the Oregon Ducks to go undefeated and win the BCS championship.

The program, run by then head coach Gene Chizik, enjoyed all the benefits bestowed to title winners. Facilities improved, salaries increased, years were added to contracts and highly sought after recruits pledged their allegiance (and eligibility) to Auburn. It was impossible to think the Tigers would be anything other than elite for the foreseeable future.

But something went wrong.

A poison, laced with complacency and entitlement, worked its way into the bloodstream of the Auburn football program. Coaches began to look the other way when players were late for meetings and workouts. The culture became toxic and the work ethic that brought a championship was pitched to the side. "There was a huge lack of accountability in the weight room," said one anonymous Auburn player to Sports Illustrated's Lars Anderson. "There was this sense that 'Hey we won a national title, and we don't have to work hard.'"

In 2012, a brutal late season home loss to Texas A&M exposed the Tigers' decay to the nation. Johnny Manziel's first trip to Jordan-Hare Stadium was a laughable shellacking with the quarterback leading the Aggies to 42 first half points and 671 total yards. "I thought the program atmosphere (of Auburn's) was probably the greatest I've seen when they release the eagle and the crowd goes crazy," A&M offensive coordinator Clarence McKinney said. "But then we ran up and down the field on them. I don't feel those players really wanted to play."

Disgust from Auburn's alumni was palpable. To even consider that the talent pool was dry, especially after consecutive years of top ten recruiting classes was a notion boosters thought to be preposterous. If not the players, then blame could only fall to leadership. Fingers of condemnation moved into the face of Gene Chizik. Pillars of Auburn football – discipline, hard work and astute reinforcement – had disappeared under the embattled head coach. Those in charge of decisions at Auburn believed Chizik no longer possessed the ability or desire to bring the Tigers back. He was unceremoniously fired and the search for Auburn's next head coach led them to a familiar face.

Gus Malzahn had spent three years as the Tigers' offensive coordinator under Chizik. Leaving the program after 2011 to take the head coaching job at Arkansas State, Malzahn took noticeable interest in the

112

possibility of returning to Auburn and coaching in the SEC. For the officials at Auburn, Malzahn was the perfect candidate because he was known around the country as a progressive and innovative offensive mind and it certainly did not hurt that without him, the 2012 Auburn offense languished in the lower half of the nation in points and yards gained. Once interest was shared from both sides, the relationship was consummated with a multi-year agreement and Malzahn was named as savior to an Auburn program in shambles.

The new head coach's first action in office was to sit down with his soon-to-be seniors and ask them for their perspective on what the program needed most. The answers were universal. The players needed accountability. Malzahn ran with their advice and put the Tigers through a physical and unrelenting spring camp. "Coach Malzahn beat the crap out of us in the spring," said center Reese Dismukes. "We banged hard in the spring, and we got beat up but it was the best thing for us."

The unrelenting camp allowed Malzahn ample time to evaluate the Tigers. His suspicion that Chizik had failed to motivate a talented group of young men was confirmed as he believed Auburn's depth rivaled the best the SEC had to offer. This confidence did not extend to the position of quarterback. Malzahn feared he did not have the agile, strong-armed passer necessary to run his spread attack.

Enter Nick Marshall.

A legend in the state of Georgia for setting the all-time mark for passing touchdowns in a high school career, the once promising quarterback had fallen on hard times. Marshall first attended the University of Georgia to throw the football for head coach Mark Richt. The plan fell through when Richt felt Marshall would never outperform the talented Andy Murray. A position switch was suggested and Marshall was moved to cornerback. Miserable playing a position he was ill suited for, Marshall fell out of favor with Richt and was dismissed from the team in 2011 for an unspecified rule violation. Hoping to salvage his collegiate career, Marshall joined the team at Garden City Community College in western Kansas. It was there he caught the eye of Malzahn who was looking for a quarterback to lead Arkansas State.

Days after his move to Auburn, Malzahn's first recruiting call went to Marshall. He needed someone of Marshall's skill set to run the Tigers' offense and extended a scholarship offer to the powerful dual threat. "Auburn was the only SEC school to offer me, so it was an easy decision," Marshall said. "I wanted to finish some business in this conference."

With Malzahn calling the plays and Marshall executing them, the 2013 season had renewed hope in Auburn. "It was clear the kids had been through a storm," Malzahn said. "They had trust issues with coaches. We had to get that back. And I told them that we wouldn't judge anyone on last year's performance. I instructed my coaches to not even watch film from last year. Everyone was given a fresh start."

114

Despite an early loss to LSU, Malzahn had righted the wayward ship. Victories against Mississippi State, Ole Miss and Washington State brought the Tigers into Kyle Field as winners in five of their first six games, a single victory away from bowl eligibility.

The game against A&M had evolved for Malzahn into a series of worries over quarterbacks. His own starter, Marshall, had missed the previous week's games against Western Carolina with a knee injury. The move to hold out Marshall was implicitly made in an effort to assure the quarterback's health for Texas A&M. By judging Marshall's return to practice in the week before the face off against the Aggies, the precautionary measure appeared to be paying off. "Nick looks like he's back to normal," Malzahn said.

The necessity to have Marshall running on all cylinders could not be understated. His rapid acquisition of Malzahn's complex system had allowed Auburn's offense to improve to levels not attained since 2010. The rushing attack of Marshall and star running back Tre Mason had seen Auburn improve from 78th in the nation to 7th with just under 290 yards per game. "(Marshall) just continues to get better," Malzahn said. "He had the week off, but at the same time, he had a very good game the week before (against Ole Miss). It's just a matter of building. You can tell he's more comfortable each week with everything within our system."

Knowing Marshall was healthy permitted Malzahn to move to his next concern, stopping Johnny

Manziel. Although the Auburn defense had improved greatly in reducing the number of points allowed, the Tigers' continued to hemorrhage yards at the disastrous level of Auburn's 2012 squad. This paradox underlined the Tigers' good fortune over the first six games; a benefit Malzahn readily admitted would not be extended by Johnny Manziel. "You look at Manziel and there have been a lot of different schemes to stop him," Malzahn said. "He does a very good job of adjusting as the game goes on and taking what the defense gives him." This was the reason why having Marshall healthy was so important to Auburn's head coach. By having his offense chewing up yards and first downs, Manziel would be nothing more than a sideline observer, helpless to do anything.

The first quarter was a head spinning, delirious chunk of college football. As Auburn's dynamic duo, Marshall and Mason, danced all over the A&M front seven, Manziel was there to answer with the wide receiver many believed was on Heisman's short list, Mike Evans. Totaling 32 catches, 737 yards, five touchdowns and one heart-stopping 95 yard stiff-arm-and-score against Alabama, on the season, Evans was wreaking as much havoc as Manziel.

The nightmare of Manziel and Evans opened the game with a short pass and catch the Aggie wideout turned into six points. Weaving in and out of an Auburn defense ranked 88th in the country against the pass, Evans scored easily from 26 yards and gave Texas A&M an early 7-0 lead.

Auburn's answer to the Aggies' flashy 101 second touchdown drive, was to sandwich two scoring drives of their own around a Manziel interception. The first push of the Tigers went 86 yards with Marshall and Mason accounting for 54 of those yards. The Auburn quarterback capped the drive and tied the score with a 16 yard touchdown run. The second score came after Manziel forced a pass into heavy coverage that was picked off by Auburn defensive back Ryan Smith. The resulting drive stalled inside the A&M ten yard line and the Tigers settled for three points and a 10-7 lead.

A few weeks earlier when Nick Saban walked off Kyle Field, grateful for his Alabama's team narrow victory, the head coach spoke long and eloquently when addressing Manziel's spectacular afternoon. When asked about Evans and his 279 yards, Saban was far more direct. "He had his way with us," Saban said.

The way Evans was abusing defenses was no surprise to A&M head coach Kevin Sumlin. "You can go back to two-a-days when I said he was one of the better players in the country before the season even started," Sumlin said. "I'll stick with that. I don't think anyone would argue with that based on his performance and his consistency over the last (few) games. He's improved from a year ago from a numbers standpoint. How he approaches the game, even without the ball in his hands...it's hard to argue he's not one of the best in the country."

The wide receiver's playmaking ability was the sole reason why Auburn's 10-7 lead did not last very long. One play after connecting with Evans on an 11 yard reception, Manziel turned and fired a lateral screamer to the wide receiver. Making the catch one yard behind the line of scrimmage, Evans broke free with the help of a brilliant downfield block by the slot receiver Malcome Kennedy. Side stepping the traffic jam, Evans flashed 64 yards for his second touchdown of the quarter.

Malzahn had seen enough. As the curtain drew on an opening quarter that featured 448 total yards, 20 first downs and 24 combined points, Auburn's head coach knew his Tigers could not last in a gun battle versus Manziel and Evans. Fearing the possibility of the contest spiraling out of his control, Malzahn decided to slow the game down. Ten of the sixteen plays Auburn ran in the second quarter were of the handoff and pitch variety. The call to grind out the quarter affected both teams. Auburn was able to score early in the quarter on a Marshall third down pass to Quan Bray but failed to do anything more for the rest of the first half. A&M could only muster a game tying field goal, and for the majority of the second quarter, the teams were locked at 17.

As the clock dwindled, Auburn gave Texas A&M an opportunity to steal one final score before the halftime break. Punting from deep in his own end zone, the Tigers' Stevan Clark was slight in his effort

118

to move the football from Auburn's half of the field. His 38 yard punt allowed Manziel and Evans a chance to cash in from the Tigers' 42 yard line.

Through the 19 games of their A&M career, Manziel to Evans had accounted for 114 receptions and 1842 yards. The twosome had taken the step together from gifted freshmen to polished sophomores. What was undeniably noteworthy about the connection between the quarterback and wide receiver was their ability to read one another during Manziel's improvisations. When Manziel was on the run, Evans' ability to find open space and create a target for his quarterback was particularly impressive. "Mike Evans does a great job with throws behind him and the jump balls," Vanderbilt head coach James Franklin said. "He just makes plays. And when things are kind of a little frantic for Manziel, he throws the ball up to Mike Evans, and Mike Evans does a heck of a job making plays for him."

The clock read 36 seconds as Manziel received the exchange from center. With his receivers blanketed and the pocket caving in from the left, Manziel drifted to his right in an attempt to extend the play. Evans, stalled short in the middle of the field, broke to his left shadowing Manziel as the quarterback neared the sideline.

The threat of Manziel running up the field forced both a linebacker and cornerback from Auburn to leave their assignment in the short right flat to stop the A&M quarterback. The void, left by the two Tigers, created a perfect opening for Evans. Inhabiting the vacated area, Evans caught a soft floating pass that traveled over the heads of the rushing Tigers. The receiver tight roped along the sideline, found his footing, and drove his legs towards the goal line. As a converging Auburn defensive back closed in, Evans leapt from the three yard line, extended the football and clipped the front pylon as he was hit. The official next to the collision raised his arms signaling touchdown. The Aggies led at halftime 24-17. Evans' first half total of 182 yards was a personal best.

The Auburn offensive dry spell ended five minutes into the third quarter. Denied by a surprisingly stout A&M defense for four straight drives, the Tigers broke through with long rushes by Mason and Marshall. The runs pushed Auburn into A&M territory and a screen from Marshall to Sammie Coates tied the score at 24. The sophomore wide receiver caught the flare from Marshall, darted through the first wave of Aggie responders, and scored from 43 yards away.

A&M's answer to the Auburn touchdown was a flourish of Manziel keepers and one final scoring hookup with Evans. Rushing the ball three times for 31 yards, Manziel put the Aggie offense on Auburn's 33 yard line. After receiving the ball from center on the following second down play, Manziel once again drifted to his right. His primary target, Evans, had completed his comeback route and failed to shake the shadowing Tiger defender. The receiver and quarterback once again invented a play in the sand. With Manziel on the move, Evans ran toward the end zone, pointing high into the air, a signal for Manziel to lob the football. The pass was not soft and high as Evans hoped, but rather sharp and back toward the center third of the end zone. Evans cut his route, stutter stepped, slashed in front of the Tigers' cornerback and caught the football. The remarkable adjustment by Evans was the A&M duo's fourth touchdown of the game. The A&M lead, with four minutes left in the third, was 31-24.

Auburn brought the kickoff out to their own 40 yard line. The terrific field position was spoiled by a tactical error from Malzahn. Believing his offense might benefit from a change of pace, the head coach inserted his freshman backup quarterback Jeremy Johnson. Hoping to entice the A&M secondary into playing closer to the line due to Johnson's speed and ability to run the football, Malzahn called for a pass. The Aggies weren't fooled, and the Auburn drive was short lived, as the Tigers were held to yet another three-and-out. Manziel began the last drive of the third at his own 22 yard line.

Two huge plays, a 35 yard catch and rumble by powerful halfback Tra Carson, followed by a 25 yard scramble from Manziel, had the Aggies on the doorstep to another quick touchdown. But as quickly as A&M moved into Auburn's red zone, the drive just as rapidly evaporated. Facing a fourth down and one yard to go, Sumlin signaled for the field goal unit. Ahead seven, a successful kick would push the lead to ten, a two possession game. But another touchdown for the Aggies could arguably give them an insurmountable fourteen point lead. As the unit moved into position, Sumlin made the call to go for the kill.

The holder, punter Drew Kaser, took the snap, spun from his crouch and hit tight end Cameron Clear for three yards and a crucial first down. The crowd at Kyle Field erupted. The move was gutsy and foolish and the 87,000 in attendance loved it. Little did they know it would ultimately cost them the health of their starting quarterback.

On the first play of the fourth quarter, a second down and goal from Auburn's ten yard line, Manziel dropped back to throw. With his receivers covered, the quarterback darted up the middle. For a moment Manziel looked as if he would easily score. But inside the five yard line, Ryan White, the Tigers' cornerback who made an earlier interception, met Manziel and grabbed him around the legs. The A&M quarterback was still on his feet but losing his balance as White refused to release him. Manziel began to fall forward and extended his right arm, bent and holding the football, to break his descent. Normally Manziel would land softly on the grass and be fine but what he could not see was the now vertical Auburn defensive end LaDarius Owens leaping to help with the tackle. As Manziel's elbow contacted the turf, Owens body landed on the quarterback, driving the throwing shoulder deep into the grass. The A&M quarterback was stopped at the two yard line. After Owens slid off him, Manziel stood and knew something was terribly wrong. He made two steps toward the A&M sideline then lowered himself to the playing surface. Aggie

122

trainers rushed to the ailing signal caller as silence overtook the crowd. Matt Joeckel, the replacement starter in the season opener, began to throw and warm his arm. Two minutes passed before Johnny was helped to the sideline and then into the locker room. Joeckel threw wide of his target on third down and Lambo came back onto the field to add three points to the A&M lead. The missed opportunity to grab seven, coupled with Manziel's injury, was a loss in fortune that shifted the momentum in Auburn's favor.

If Nick Marshall was feeling the pressure it did not show. Down ten points and with a deafening A&M crowd sending decibels of hate into the earholes of his helmet, Marshall calmly advanced the Tigers down the field and cut the Aggie lead to three. The seven play, 75 yard drive was consummated with a 13 yard Marshall touchdown run three minutes into the final quarter. In the history of Auburn football, the Tigers are 298-4 when scoring over 30 points; this includes a streak of 81 straight games. The touchdown by the Auburn quarterback pushed the Tigers over the 30 point threshold but they still trailed 34-31.

The good news for A&M was that Manziel had returned from the locker room and was trying to loosen his damaged shoulder on the sideline. The bad news was every throw was an exercise in excruciating torture. Several times after Johnny tossed the football he shook his head at the A&M trainers perched anxiously at his side. When it appeared he was on the verge of stopping and calling it a day due to the pain, Manziel gritted his teeth and made another throw.

With all the attention on Manziel, Joeckel returned to the game and failed to move the chains. Hampered by an early false start penalty, the Aggies were forced to kick the ball back to the reinvigorated Tiger offense.

Answering the call on first and second down, the A&M defense forced Auburn into a short third down. With one yard needed, the Aggies loaded the line in an effort to hold the Tigers. Malzahn called for a handoff to Mason. The shifty running back took the football and broke through the line. Failing to be tackled by the leaning Aggie defense, Mason was free to run, taking the football 53 yards to the A&M seven yard line. Two plays later, a shocked Kyle Field crowd watched Cameron Artis-Payne cross the goal line. Without Manziel, a ten point lead had evaporated into a four point deficit.

Watching the A&M defense surrender his lead forced Manziel to will his injured shoulder into shape. Refusing to standby and observe, the A&M quarterback ran onto the field to a roaring, relieved ovation. The first pass of his return went naturally to Evans. One play and the Aggies were in Auburn territory. With the clock just under nine minutes, there was little need to move hurriedly but in deference to a shoulder he wasn't sure would last, Manziel moved the Aggies along at a brisk pace.

The A&M quarterback looked crisp and strong with his throws, answering the concerns of the worried

Aggie faithful who could not believe the return of their signal caller after witnessing Manziel's discomfort on the sideline. "Johnny is like Superman out there," A&M wide receiver Malcome Kennedy said. "I heard him talking to the coaches and the trainers, saying he had to go back into the game. That's just his spirit, and to see him be a leader like that and play through pain, it motivates us as a team to play harder."

Manziel crossed the fifty yard line and dissected the Auburn defense in ten plays, converting two third downs and removing four minutes from the clock. A one yard touchdown sneak by Manziel returned the lead to Texas A&M. The quarterback's fifth touchdown made the score 41-38.

With a three point lead and a game clock that read just over five minutes remaining, the Aggie defense was searching for the midgame magic that held Auburn in check. But Auburn's final drive of the game was a cluster of near misses presenting the Aggies with numerous opportunities to stop Marshall and Mason but ultimately helpless to throw a knockout punch. On the first set of downs, A&M forced a third down and three to go. Marshall rushed for four yards. Two plays later, another third down was converted when Mason rushed for seven yards when four was needed. The final third down conversion was perhaps the most important play of the game. Facing a third and nine on the Aggie 39 yard line, Marshall faked a handoff to Mason and wedged a pass into coverage to his tight end, Marcus Davis, for a gain of 27 yards. Two plays after the Davis' clutch catch, Mason crossed the goal line on a five yard run and Auburn's lead was restored, 45-41.

Malzahn looked to the clock and although he was pleased to own the lead he wished the clock had fewer than its 79 remaining seconds. The head coach deeply feared it was too much time to give a quarterback like Manziel. Adding insult to injury Sumlin also had all three timeouts at his disposal. All the Auburn coach could hope for was his defense to make one last stand.

The quarterback, racked with pain, grimaced as he trotted onto Kyle Field. The Aggies started 65 yards from the goal line thanks to Trey Williams' 35 yard kick return. Nineteen yards were gained on the drive's first play, a bullet to Evans, the wideout's tenth catch of the contest. Hurrying to the spot of the ball, Auburn's 46 yard line, Manziel called his own number. The resulting six yard rush did not stop the clock, now under 60 seconds left. On second down, Manziel made his eleventh connection with Evans, a 22 yard catch, and in a breathless 36 seconds, the Aggies were on Auburn's 18 yard line.

Malzahn called timeout.

With the clock stopped at 43 seconds, Manziel had the remaining time plus three timeouts to enter the end zone. Opportunity certainly lied in attacking the middle of the field, possibly utilizing a secondary receiver such as Kennedy, or last week's hero Travis Labhart. But on first down Manziel chose neither as he dropped back and threw to the double covered Evans. The throw was off target, toward the back shoulder of the wideout. Evans had to jump, twist, and extend his right arm just to make play on the ball. The pass struck Evans in the palm of his right hand and bounced away through the back of the end zone. The back judge ruled the pass incomplete.

Evans, who had eleven receptions and a school record 287 yards, was beside himself. Angry at his inability to make the catch, the wide receiver stormed to the huddle determined to win the game.

He would never get the chance.

The Tigers sacked Manziel on second down and then again on fourth down.

Evans ran off the field and did not stop.

He did not need to watch Auburn kneel and kill the remainder of the game. The result would be the same.

The Aggies had lost their second game of the season.

9 Vanderbilt & UTEP

In the wake of the soul crushing defeat to Auburn, Texas A&M players and coaches took turns assigning and accepting blame.

Mike Evans, inconsolable moments after the final seconds disappeared from the Auburn game, refused to speak immediately to the media. Later in the week, after the loss soaked in, Evans pointed the finger at himself even though he posted numbers never seen by a pass catcher at A&M. Disheartened by his failed attempt to make the twisting circus catch at the end of the game Evans said, "I just knew that was the last chance. I should have just high pointed the ball. There were two guys there. I didn't think fast enough."

Shouldering perhaps the largest beast of self-blame was A&M defensive coordinator Mark Snyder. The stellar performance in the middle of the game by the Aggie defense was overshadowed by a disastrous fourth quarter. Auburn rushed for 168 yards and converted all four of their third downs in the final stanza. "We had a stretch where we felt like we were comfortable with the game," Snyder said. "I thought we were playing pretty well. When they had to move the football and they had to move the chains, they did. Good defense doesn't allow that to happen. When you score 41 points, you should win. End of story."

Others were damning the luck of Johnny Manziel's injury. The timing of the injury could not have been worse. After A&M's successful fake field goal early in the fourth, the computers at ESPN gave Auburn less than a 9% chance of winning. Manziel was hurt two plays later and the backup quarterback, Matt Joeckel, failed to cross the goal line on third down. Instead of seven, the A&M offense settled for three. The four point swing was the difference in the game. Even with missing a series early in the final quarter, the A&M starter gained 454 passing and 48 rushing yards. The total was Manziel's fifth game of over 500 yards of total offense. A staggering achievement to consider as no one in the history of the SEC had previously accomplished the feat more than once.

The post-game MRI on Manziel's shoulder revealed no structural damage. Doctors recommended the A&M quarterback immobilize the joint with a sling. No one could tell Manziel when he would be back, ready to play. This lack of clarity stoked the fire of rumor. On Monday, when Manziel showed up to practice in the sling, reports began to spring from the belly of the internet claiming the quarterback would miss three weeks and would not play the remainder of the home stand. Kevin Sumlin did little to define the duration of Manziel's possible vacation when the coach could only offer that he was "hopeful" to see his starter play on Saturday against Vanderbilt.

Laughably, the lone definitive voice in the debate of will-he-or-won't-he came from Commodores head coach James Franklin. Asked at his weekly press conference if he believed Manziel would start, Franklin said, "Well, Manziel's playing. I don't think there's any doubt or question about that whatsoever. He's going to be fine. I think he's got like titanium bones."

Franklin wanted to dismiss the Manziel rumors because his team needed to focus on what was a tough but winnable game. Vanderbilt was headed to Kyle Field with a short gust of momentum as the Commodores were part of the previous week's massacre on the AP Top 25 with their 31-27 defeat of No. 15 Georgia. Even with Manziel, the Aggies had lost four games on their home field over the past two seasons, a peculiar vulnerability in the era of Johnny Football.

Sumlin could not share Franklin's confidence because he simply did not have a read on whether or not Manziel would be healthy enough to play. In addition to Monday, the quarterback missed Tuesday, Wednesday, and Thursday's practice and was only able to endure a light, no-pads, thirty minute throwing session on Friday. The workout was so cautious no one, including Manziel, had any further inclination to the quarterback's availability. Complicating matters even more was the early 11 A.M. kickoff on Saturday. Manziel would have to test the shoulder far earlier than normal on a game day.

Manziel woke on Saturday with a stiff shoulder. The soreness, a byproduct of the five days in the sling, was pronounced as kickoff crept closer. Undeterred by the pain, Manziel found Sumlin roaming the field during pregame warm-ups and told his coach he was ready to play. "In my mind I was always going to play," Manziel said after the game. "It would take a lot to keep me off the field and away from these guys. These guys count on me and they expect me to be there, so if I have to come in and get treatment or whatever I have to do to get back, I have to do it for these guys."

What Manziel did for the Aggie offense was undeniable. Sensing the Commodores may be expecting a heavy dose of runs to compensate and protect Manziel's shoulder, A&M offensive coordinator Clarence McKinney peppered Vanderbilt early with passes. Showing nothing to make one think his throwing motion was hampered, Manziel completed his first ten throws, torching the Commodore defense for three first quarter touchdowns. The A&M quarterback found wide receivers Derel Walker, LaQuivonte Gonzalez and Mike Evans on the touchdown passes. The last throw to Evans, a gorgeous 43 yard fade route that hit the wideout in stride, was Manziel's best pass of the day. Heading into the second quarter with a 21-0 lead extinguished any concerns Manziel would tamper with the potency of A&M's offense.

Vanderbilt's offense, however, was struggling, because unlike A&M, the Commodores had to replace their injured starting quarterback. Freshman Patton Robinette, in for senior Austyn Carta Samuels, was forced into incompletions and sacks by an energetic A&M defense. Backfield takedowns of Robinette, by Aggie defensive end Gavin Stansbury and linebacker Steven Jenkins, contributed to three consecutive punts the Aggie offense converted into touchdowns. "Starting out three-and-out against a high-powered opponent, (is) not the way you want to start the game on offense knowing that you're going to have to score some points to win this game," Franklin said in the postgame news conference. The third punt by the Commodores gave Manziel a short field to work with and five plays after the kick the Aggies trotted into the end zone with their fourth touchdown of the game. Running back Trey Williams' 11 yard rush pushed the A&M lead to 28-0.

Down but certainly not out, the Vanderbilt quarterback found his rhythm in the second quarter. A period after gaining a meager 40 yards, the Commodores closed the deficit to eleven with a 30 yard touchdown pass to Jordan Matthews, a four yard scoring run by Jerron Seymour and a 23 yard field goal by Casey Spear.

The Aggies ended the first half with a whimper in light of their commanding open. A&M failed to add to their lead due to an unsuccessful fourth down conversion, a Manziel interception and a Trey Williams fumble. The poor performance to close the second quarter lit a fuse under A&M's senior running back Ben Malena. Feeling that the Aggies had become

132

sloppy after building the large lead, Malena took it upon himself to voice a raving displeasure to his teammates. Sumlin felt the same way. Sequestered to an office, the head coach went over adjustments with assistants and warned them he was about to light a fire under his players. He was too late. Entering the locker room, Sumlin listened as Malena demanded an improved effort in the second half and shouted, "Let's go!" The head coach realized there was no need for additional motivation. He looked into the hungry group and said, "All right, what he said."

The Aggies ran from the locker room and tore into the Commodores as Robinette's first pass of the third quarter was intercepted and returned for a touchdown. Junior safety Howard Matthews stepped in front of the freshman's throw and ran 26 yards for A&M's fifth touchdown of the day. A blizzard of punts and fumbles took place over the next six minutes, a comedy of errors that concluded when Manziel found Walker in the end zone for the wideout's second touchdown of the game. The extra point made the score 42-17 in favor of the Aggies and Manziel's day was over.

Although the A&M quarterback was through playing against Vanderbilt, he was not through making news. Toward the end of the game, the video board at Kyle Field played a new episode of "Ask the Aggies." The segment shows responses by A&M players to silly, lighthearted questions. For the Vanderbilt game, the question posed to the players was "Who would you like to have as a party guest?" Manziel answered he

133

would most like to enjoy the company of actor Charlie Sheen, New England Patriots tight end (and renowned party animal) Rob Gronkowski and after a pause, the quarterback added Tiger Woods. The answers, harmless and good for a chuckle, were the basis for a stupefying debate the following morning on ESPN.com. College football analysts Jesse Palmer and Danny Kanell, both former quarterbacks at elite programs, discussed their perception that the answers Manziel gave on the video were indicative of a larger immaturity A&M officials needed to control. Palmer, a former contestant on ABC's dating show The Bachelor, was defiant in his opinion that Manziel was not ready for the next level and needed refinement. Coming from a man who believed he could find his wife in six weeks in front of a national audience, Palmer's opinion of Manziel appeared to be disingenuous at best.

In spite of the argument as to what Manziel should be off the field, his play against Vanderbilt went just as the doctor ordered. The quarterback, limited to a season low three carries, only experienced two soft sacks by the Commodores. "It wasn't really in our game plan this week for me to run," said Manziel. The slight physical toll he endured in the 56-24 A&M victory was cause for restrained celebration. "My shoulder is just a little sore," Manziel said. "I don't know if it's bruised or what's going on. I kind of got squished when I went down last week against Auburn. It didn't cause me too many problems today, so that was positive."

134

What was causing Manziel problems was not his ailing shoulder but an offense he believed had lost its' confidence. The Aggies turned the ball over five times against Vanderbilt and although a few A&M coaches and players dismissed the giveaways as mere hiccups, Manziel believed it was a sign of a significant fracture. The quarterback, blaming the debilitating loss to Auburn for the deep slice, felt helpless in the weeks afterward. "Auburn was the one that stung for a long time, especially offensively," Manziel said in December as the Aggies prepared for their bowl game. "Just going from that game and kind of transitioning to some other ones and some nonconference games thrown in there, we just kind of lost our confidence after that and never really could get it back."

The fissure Manziel feared was tearing the A&M offense apart was never more prevalent than in the first quarter of A&M's game against UTEP. The Miners from El Paso, winners of only one game in 2013, had compelled the Aggies to punt the ball away three times in their first four possessions. Manziel stormed the sideline after the punt team was sent onto the field to conclude the fourth possession.

Echoing Ben Malena's call to arms during halftime against Vanderbilt, Manziel asked for the lethargic Aggie offense to surround him. He looked into the eyes of his lineman, his running backs, his receivers, and told them the effort they had shown thus far was unacceptable. "Johnny called us over as a unit, the whole offensive team, and just gave a great leadership speech," said senior wideout Travis Labhart

135

who was responsible at the moment of the speech for A&M's lone first quarter touchdown. "I think he did a good job of assuming the leadership role and taking charge and letting us know that we needed to pick up what we were doing."

The speech galvanized Manziel and his receivers. A 23 yard completion to Malcome Kennedy set up A&M's second touchdown of the game. Then, after a DeVante Harris interception, Manziel connected once again with Kennedy for a 15 yard touchdown. The reception by Kennedy was Manziel's 50th career touchdown pass.

Resurrection of a dormant A&M offense was aided by an exuberant, swarming Aggie defense. By suffocating the UTEP run game, the Aggie front seven teed off on the Miners' quarterback through a barrage of exotic blitzes. The second giveaway, a fumble recovered by A&M cornerback Noel Ellis, was turned into six points on a diving ten yard touchdown run by Manziel. The following UTEP possession ended when Howard Matthews intercepted a pass Manziel later converted into Labhart's second touchdown grab of the game. The 28 yard score blew the game wide open as the Aggies led at halftime, 36-7.

Johnny Manziel opened the scoring in the second half with a run that ranked amongst the quarterback's best during his time at A&M. After receiving the snap, Manziel darted through a hole along the left side of the offensive line. Carrying the ball in his right hand, as if he could throw at any moment, the quarterback rounded his run back to the center of the field to avoid UTEP's secondary. It was there Manziel was met by several helping Miners looking to make the tackle, so he fled back to the left. Untouched as he zigged, then zagged, Manziel crossed the goal line after beginning 49 yards away. The touchdown was A&M's longest run of the season.

Continuing its' stingy front, the A&M defense quickly put the ball back into Manziel's hands so the quarterback could right his final perceived wrong. With the game firmly on cruise control, the A&M quarterback hoped to use his final drive to reconnect with Evans. Targeting the receiver six times in the first half yet failing to complete a single of those attempts, Manziel hoped to reestablish his link to Evans as the Aggies neared the end zone. The A&M quarterback dropped back and threw a strike Evans easily corralled for a 26 yard touchdown. A&M's lead stood at 50-7.

The Aggie offense scored six touchdowns on six straight possessions following the sideline rant by Manziel. In 38 minutes of football, Manziel had matched his career high with six touchdowns – 4 passing, 2 rushing – and totaled 340 yards of total offense. The A&M quarterback hoped the worst was behind them. They were supposed to manhandle the UTEP's of the world, yet their early struggles against the Miners, coupled with the mistakes against Vanderbilt, made the Aggie offense appear mortal. A terrifying proposition to consider when taking into account the vulnerabilities of the young Aggie defense.

Overwhelming their considerable flaws was the only way A&M could finish their shrinking season in glory. Manziel certainly believed it could be done, regardless of the crumbling façade that urged him to think otherwise. Four games remained. The first, a home game against Mississippi State, was the final contest at Kyle Field for the 2013 season. The afternoon game would be a farewell to the seniors' playing career in College Station and the current version of Kyle Field, as the stadium was due for a nine figure offseason facelift. Those departures were assured, but the 12th Man had to wonder, would those be the only ones to say goodbye?

10 Mississippi State

Before the 2013 season was underway, Johnny Manziel was the most polarizing of the 2014 draft prospects. Appraisals of the young quarterback varied from complaints about the passer's size (or rather lack of), to complimentary reports that praised his innate abilities. Those who disliked Manziel were concerned about his off-the-field baggage. "You build a franchise around high level people as much as high-level players," said a former Philadelphia Eagles scout. The statement was a jab at the perception Manziel did not fit into the former category nearly as well as he did in the latter. Scouts sharing this conviction felt the A&M quarterback was a project in the NFL, worth no more than a third round selection.

Manziel's dedication to improving his accuracy, and his pocket presence paid off in games like Alabama, Auburn, and the comeback win over Ole Miss. The A&M quarterback was looking more and more like an NFL quarterback. Those same scouts that believed Manziel was a risky prospect in August now felt in November that he was one of the top passers of the 2014 crop of quarterbacks. "He reminds me a little bit of Joe Montana," one NFL scout told the

Milwaukee Journal Sentinel. "(Manziel's) fluid and even though he's off balance he can get the ball out."

Current and former NFL quarterbacks began to share their opinions in the Manziel draft debate. The main focus of discussion centered on Manziel's height. Although Manziel was listed at six feet, one inch, there were many that believed the quarterback was shorter. This was a serious problem for NFL front offices that wanted the prototypical six feet, four inch, 230 pound passer. Luckily for Manziel the issue was not nearly the kiss of death it was a decade ago. A rash of successful and shorter NFL passers had made the steadfast opinion of what a quarterback should be change over the past several seasons. The most popular passer to go against this stereotype was the Super Bowl winning quarterback of the New Orleans Saints', Drew Brees. Standing at six feet tall, Brees liked Manziel's chances to one day be an NFL starter. "He's a heck of a player," Brees told foxsports.com. "He makes all kinds of plays. He's got all the playmaking ability to be a great player. (There are) guys like (Manziel) in this league."

Analysts were suggesting Manziel had firmly played his way into the first round, a threshold that was significant in the quarterback's mind. He had two years of eligibility remaining at A&M and regardless of the grind that sometimes surrounded Johnny he wasn't willing to forfeit the opportunity to stay and improve as a quarterback, on the hope and prayer of going in the first round. He would have to be sure that he was going to be drafted early. "I don't want to be a guy that has a first round grade and come out and go into second round," Manziel told Andy Staples of Sports Illustrated. "That's the difference between $12 million and $4 million or $5 million. That's still a lot of money obviously, but not when you have two full years left on the table."

According to Wright Thompson's ESPN profile of Manziel, there was another factor affecting Johnny's decision to turn pro. In the days and weeks after the Heisman, time that ultimately stretched into the summer, the relationship between the Manziel family and the university became strained. Allegations from the Manziel's ran the gauntlet, from the belief that the school leaked a story about Johnny almost transferring after his 2012 arrest, to the opinion A&M officials withheld the quarterback's copy of the Heisman so the university could milk the additional statue for fundraising purposes. The perceived transgressions left a sour taste in the family's mouth.

Efforts were made from the university to repair the split. One of the Manziel family's chief complaints against A&M was they did not seem interested in shielding Johnny from the intrusion of the NCAA. This problem was certainly remedied during the August investigation. Chancellor John Sharp's staunch defense of Manziel was key to the reduction in punishment Johnny endured. The breach between the two parties had softened, and a begrudging respect had taken its' place.

The relationship appeared to be on the mend. Even more surprising was the development that Johnny was beginning to relax in the bubble of College Station. "I think I've absolutely been able to enjoy myself," Manziel said. "I've had a great time in College Station this year, had a great group of friends, a great group of teammates that have been around me since things kind of changed back in August. But life's been good. I've been able to enjoy things in College Station. It's really mellowed out a lot and I've been able to go more places and do more. It really has been a great year. I've enjoyed every second of it."

Knowing there remained a fighting chance to keep Manziel around made the university's rebuttal to a late season article claiming Johnny Manziel's celebrity stature had contributed millions in donations to the school all the more puzzling. If the athletic department hoped Manziel would stay for his junior year, then why were they doing everything they could to refuse his importance? With the biggest decision of Manziel's life on the horizon, a choice that would greatly affect Texas A&M, it seemed a strange time to begin a war of denials.

Bloomberg.com, the website extension of the renowned financial media outlet, expanded its' reach into the sports world several years ago. Creating a spinoff that dabbled in the money side of the athletic world, Bloomberg Sports was anxious to delve into the Manziel controvery back in August, but instead chose to carefully put together a report hoping to answer just what a Heisman Trophy winner brought to a university.

142

Their findings were sprung upon Aggieland as College Station was preparing to say goodbye to their seniors and hoping to convince Johnny Football to stay another year.

At the heart of the report were undisputable facts. In the fiscal year 2013, running September 2012 through August 2013, Texas A&M University had raised, through pledges and donations, a staggering $740 million dollars. Close to $300 million more than the university brought in over the 2012 fiscal year. When asked about the surge in funds and how that related to the arrival of Manziel, officials in the A&M athletic department pointed to the perfect storm of the move to the SEC, the Kyle Field renovation, and the new television deals brought by the conference change. "People draw the conclusion that we made millions from Johnny winning the Heisman," said A&M Athletic Director Eric Hyman. "I'd say we've gotten more financial benefit from joining what's widely perceived as the best football conference in the country and having a winning program." When pressed for a dollar amount, school officials were reported to have said Manziel brought $20,000 to the university through an auction where the high bidder was allowed to dine with the quarterback at a football fundraising dinner. Denying Manziel's contribution was a peculiar stance to take considering how the university responded in the days after the quarterback's historic Heisman win.

When Johnny Manziel won the Heisman in December of 2012, the athletic department created a six figure advertising campaign to highlight the quarterback's win.   A billboard was immediately purchased for Times Square in New York City with the slogan "Call him Johnny Heisman" accompanied by the Texas A&M logo. The university released a report stating "research conducted by Joyce Julius & Associates shows that the redshirt freshman winning the prestigious trophy produced more than 1.8 million media impressions, which translates into $37 million in media exposure for Texas A&M. An A&M official went even farther, estimating Manziel's financial impact for Texas A&M would rival the fundraising haul Robert Griffin III's Heisman winning career brought Baylor University. A figure believed to be around $250 million.

That was all weeks after Manziel's Heisman win. Months later the tune changed dramatically.

Texas A&M Foundations' Mark Klemm told Bloomberg that the increase in fundraising for Kyle Field's remodel had no tie to Manziel's win. "You can't remotely say that," Klemm said. "The planning for the stadium started before we joined the SEC and before Johnny Manziel became our starting quarterback.   It was just an amazing coincidence of timing." The company line both indirectly and directly from the school was that Manziel's personal triumphs were inconsequential. A perspective that rankled the 12th Man. Fan outcry flooded the internet and forced an A&M official to issue a statement on a popular Texas A&M message board with the admittance that "Johnny has certainly been a major component and catalyst of our tremendous growth." The confession

144

was met with derision. It made little sense to insult the individual most responsible for the meteoric rise of Texas A&M. The timing of the rudeness by university officials, especially so close to the conclusion of the season and within range of Manziel's decision, was seen as amateurish and without tact.

After the spectators left from A&M's final 2013 home game, Kyle Field would experience a major facelift. The field would be lowered seven feet, 15,000 seats would be added, and the east side of the stadium would be enclosed. The renovation, at a cost of $450 million, would put Kyle Field in the realm of college football's greatest stadiums. "It'll be a historic moment for the players and fans," said Kevin Sumlin. "After Saturday, Kyle Field will look completely different forever. The ability to play in that game for everybody, coach in that game or be a fan at that game to me, is a big deal. It's a really historic moment." Perhaps the seniors who would be playing their final game in College Station were focused on the history of the stadium and personal reflections upon their football career. The rest were wondering if this was the last time Johnny Manziel would play on Kyle Field.

If the A&M quarterback was carrying the burden of his future decision or the face slap provided by an ungrateful university, he did not show it to Mississippi State. Manziel was responsible for 196 of the 203 yards the Aggies gained in the first quarter. On the Aggies' first touchdown drive, Manziel was surgical, completing all four passes to two receivers – Malcome Kennedy and Travis Labhart. Set up by a stop of Mississippi State on fourth down, the drive started with a 12 yard sideline pass from Manziel to Kennedy. The ball, now at midfield, went to Labhart next. Lined up in the slot, the senior wideout caught the play action pass from Manziel for 15 yards. The quarterback added two rushes for 21 yards before finding Kennedy for the touchdown. The 12 yard scoring strike started with the wide receiver lined up in a tight three receiver formation to Manziel's left. The quarterback received the center exchange and was flushed left by a strong Mississippi State rush. Kennedy broke to the center of the end zone where Manziel floated a soft pass the wideout ran under, making the catch, and giving A&M the first score of the game.

Texas A&M has one of college football's oldest tradition's in the 12th Man. Every year the coaching staff chooses a walk-on player to play special teams and wear the number 12 signifying the role of the student body's support to the program. Occasionally, the 12th Man will rise and make a terrific play. After the Bulldogs tied the game at seven, the 12th Man for 2013, Sam Moeller, blocked a punt through the back of the end zone to give A&M a 9-7 lead. The free kick from Mississippi State was returned to A&M's 38 yard line and the stage for the Aggies' second touchdown was set.

146

Travis Labhart did not become a weapon for Johnny Manziel until A&M receivers coach David Beatty suggested a slight position adjustment during the Ole Miss game to Kevin Sumlin. "I said, 'Coach, I'm going to make a change, and I'm going to Lab in the H, and he'll be fine,'" Beatty told Joshua Siegel of the *Eagle*. "He looked back at me and said, 'He'll be great. Put him in there. Let's roll.'" The move paid immediate dividends for the Aggies as Labhart was the chief outlet for Manziel in the comeback win, but long term, the wide receiver had become irreplaceable. 24 receptions in the past four games, including the two touchdown performance against UTEP, had elevated the wide receiver to a finalist for the Burlsworth Trophy given to the year's best player that began his career as a walk-on.

The final possession of the first quarter for A&M started with a 14 yard reception by Kennedy that advanced the ball to midfield. An incompletion and short run by Ben Malena forced A&M into a third down and long. Manziel took the snap and moved to his left. Against his body he threw to Labhart and the wideout made the catch for fifteen yards, good for a drive sustaining first down.

The touchdown came on the following play. With three receivers clustered to his right, Manziel took the snap and dropped back into the pocket. The receivers raced up the field, then two broke to the sideline. The third, Labhart, patiently waited for the pair of wideouts to clear and then sprinted toward the middle of the field. The Bulldogs' cornerback and safety in the area jumped the dual out routes, leaving Labhart alone. Manziel threw a bullet to the senior wideout that Labhart caught at the Mississippi State five yard line. A vicious hit from a Bulldog defender carried the receiver into the end zone. The first quarter ended with A&M leading 16-7.

The first four drives of the second quarter ended in punts. These failed attempts to score would usually not warrant a mention, but on Texas A&M's second drive of the quarter, Manziel tried to hit Mike Evans on a deep pass. As the quarterback followed through with his right arm, his throwing hand struck the top of a lineman's helmet. Manziel immediately recoiled and grabbed the center of his pain, his right thumb. He did not leave the game. However, it was an injury that would affect the quarterback for the remainder of the regular season.

A nice 50 yard punt by A&M's Drew Kaser out of the Aggies' own end zone was nullified by a 15 yard facemask penalty on the run back. Mississippi State took advantage of the short field, scoring in five plays, to close the A&M advantage to two points.

With less than a minute before halftime, Manziel brought A&M out of their second quarter hibernation, despite the distressed thumb. A 16 yard run by the signal caller followed by a seven yard screen to Malena moved A&M to midfield as the clock dropped under 40 seconds. On first down from the A&M 48, Manziel took advantage of another blown coverage by the Bulldogs. Running a route along the left sideline, Derel Walker snuck behind a distracted

Mississippi State cornerback. Manziel lofted a perfect pass to the wide open Walker, who took the catch to the Bulldogs' 11 yard line. A&M signaled for a timeout with 20 seconds before the break.

Manziel was backpedaling on the next play, not yet through with his drop into the pocket, when he threw a pass to the slashing Labhart. The senior made the catch and entered the end zone with ease. The four play, 75 yard drive lasted 41 seconds.

The Bulldogs' knelt the remainder of the first half away, looking at a 23-14 disadvantage.

Manziel was not perfect for the home crowd. He was intercepted once, midway through the first quarter, a poor decision as the Aggies were set to score. Imperfection reared its' ugly head again on A&M's first possession of the second half. After being gifted a retry when Mississippi State roughed Kaser to give Manziel a fresh set of downs, the quarterback wasted the opportunity with a terrible pass behind a falling Kennedy that was intercepted. Fortunately the Bulldogs could not capitalize as Evan Sobiesk missed a 40 yard field goal and A&M's lead remained at nine.

A&M would add two more touchdowns before the horn sounded on the third quarter. The first scoring drive began and ended with receptions by Malcome Kennedy. A 17 yard catch by the junior wide receiver was followed by another big catch from Labhart. The 26 yard reception set up Kennedy's touchdown. With the ball on the Bulldogs' 21 yard line, Manziel eluded the grasp of a Mississippi State defender, rolled right, and hit Kennedy in the end zone for his fourth touchdown pass of the day.

Mississippi State answered later in the quarter with their own touchdown drive, a 96 yard beauty that cut the A&M lead to ten. The score began a manic three minute exchange where both teams traded two touchdowns each.

The final A&M touchdown of the third came on the back of Manziel's most explosive play of the game, a 75 yard catch and run by Evans. The monstrous gain was created by another mistake from a Bulldog defensive back. This time the cornerback, unsure if he was to blitz Manziel, became frozen in confusion. Evans slid around the baffled defender, caught the Manziel pass and ran to Mississippi State's 15 yard line. Running back Trey Williams scored on the next play, expanding A&M's advantage as the third quarter ended, to seventeen.

The Bulldogs opened the fourth with a 31 yard touchdown pass to Joe Morrow. A score that was answered by A&M three plays later when Manziel threw his fifth and final touchdown to the seldom used senior tight end Nehemiah Hicks.

The 28 point avalanche covered over 250 yards in eight plays, a dizzying back and forth that did not change A&M's lead.

Mississippi State's chances at crawling back into the game disappeared when an A&M interception was turned into a one yard touchdown run by Ben Malena. With under eleven minutes left, and the score standing in favor of A&M at 51-27, the student body began to chant a clear and direct message to Manziel.

They wanted one more year.

Manziel was feast and famine against the Bulldogs, tying his personal best in touchdown passes and interceptions. He finished seven yards shy of another 500 yard game in total offense and became the only quarterback in the last ten years of the SEC to throw for four touchdowns in four straight games. If this was to be the end of his career at Kyle Field then he did not spoil the opportunity to put on a show.

As the curtain fell upon A&M's 51-41 victory, Manziel ran across the field, jumped into the students' section, and sang the traditional Aggie War Hymn. Grinning as he wrapped his arms around his fellow classmates, Manziel sang with the passion of someone who might never get the chance to sing the Aggie War Hymn again.

Manziel was slow to leave the playing surface. His family, perched close to the tunnel leading to the A&M locker room, waited for the quarterback. On the videoboard, Manziel's Heisman acceptance speech played. If he was to leave school for the NFL, the decision would not be free of emotion for anyone in the family. As the speech played, tears welled up in the eyes of Manziel's mother. It had been a long journey, one that had changed their lives forever.

The quarterback made a stop to greet his family. He hugged his mother, shook hands, and took a long last look at Kyle Field for the season.

"It was really emotional and really awesome, and it really speaks volumes to how awesome the student body is and this fan base and how special everything about Texas A&M is," Manziel said. "It's a really special place and I love it here."

11 LSU & Mizzou

It is rare for a college football team to pass through a full season unscathed. In the eight seasons from 2006-2013 only three teams have won the BCS championship with an undefeated record. Knowing your beloved team will most likely lose, over the course of thirteen regular season games, does not lessen the sting when defeat inevitably occurs. For many diehard alumni these losses cut deep and the unending wounds last many generations.

Before the season, there was a collective dream in College Station that 2013 would end with Kevin Sumlin and Johnny Manziel celebrating upon a stage as waves of floating confetti kissed their skin. They would be given the trophy of the BCS championship, a crystal football, to raise high into the air. In the long months before football began, this vision of greatness brought an insatiable hunger onto tongues that bleed maroon. Seduced by Manziel's Heisman and the fortunes of their initial SEC season, the Aggie nation, known as the 12th Man, created an expectation of certainty.

It was not meant to be.

153

Setbacks to Alabama and Auburn extinguished the fire of hope that burned through the spring and summer months. Making those failures even harder to digest was that both heart wrenching defeats happened on the grass of Kyle Field. But for those gifted few that are able to quickly forget the past, lies the opportunity of redemption. Battle scarred teams cling to this adage and to the truism that renewal springs eternal in the week leading to Saturday's game.

The Aggies, riding the goodwill of their current four game winning streak, were making the case to their fans and to the nation that they had overcome their distant failures. Perched at No. 12 in the BCS rankings, Texas A&M was in position to restore faith with wins in their final two games. The path to salvaging the season would not be without obstacle, but there were believers who contended the Aggies could find their way to a Sugar Bowl or perhaps even help their quarterback lift a second bronze statue.

To turn dreams into realities, Texas A&M would have to do something only one team in the last thirty games had accomplished. Their mission would entail traveling to Baton Rouge and defeating LSU in the hornet's nest known as Death Valley.

The central spark igniting the renewed imagination of the Aggie faithful was the undeniable truth that Johnny Manziel was back in the Heisman chase. The 493 yard performance against Mississippi

154

State certainly refreshed voters' minds to the remarkable talents of the Aggie quarterback, but it was a nasty piece of legal business going on in Tallahassee, Florida that had many wondering if Manziel might win by default. Florida State quarterback and Heisman frontrunner, Jameis Winston, was named in an ESPN report as being the focus of an investigation alleging sexual assault. The victim reported that after a night of drinking at a bar in Tallahassee, she was taken back to Winston's apartment where the alleged assault took place. As lawyers argued over police suppression, DNA results, and a myriad of other stomach churning details, those who dealt in the trade of college football analysis began to debate if Manziel was worthy of an accomplishment not seen since Ohio State running back Archie Griffin enjoyed back to back Heisman wins in 1974 and 1975.

Looking at the numbers Manziel had posted through the first ten games, it was hard to deny he had markedly improved. His touchdown passes stood at 31, an improvement of 13 from the same point last season. He led the nation in completion percentage from within the pocket, completions of over 20 yards, and his 9.6 yards per attempt while throwing on the run was four yards better than average. "From an intangible standpoint...from an ability to make throws, (Manziel) worked as hard as any quarterback I've ever seen," said Kirk Herbstreit, ESPN analyst and former Ohio State quarterback.

Revenge lurked in Manziel's heart. In 2012, the LSU Tigers bewildered the electric quarterback, handing the streaking Aggies a 24-19 loss at Kyle Field. Manziel was disappointing in the defeat, gaining only 27 rushing yards and completing a career low 52% of his passes. Tigers defensive coordinator John Chavis created a containment scheme forcing Manziel to stay in the pocket. Instead of using his defensive ends in a variety of blitzes, Chavis had them perform one simple task. Rush Manziel vertically. This meant the ends moved in a straight line up the field creating an outside boundary the A&M quarterback could not slide around. The defensive approach kept Manziel out of the end zone and frustrated him into three interceptions.

But these Tigers, the 2013 version, were not as talented or effective as the group that stifled Manziel a year ago. Even though LSU was the lone defeat on Auburn's schedule, the Tigers had been beat by Georgia, Ole Miss and Alabama. In each of those losses the defense had surrendered huge plays and out of character point totals. Despite evidence to the contrary, LSU head coach Les Miles believed his defense would play well for the home crowd. "I want the defense to stop them," Miles said. "Certainly we recognize the challenge an offense like A&M will bring...I like my defense. I suspect they'll play best in this game. I think they'll be a challenge to A&M and I think being in Tiger Stadium will be a challenge to A&M. It's a much different environment and a place where the home team generally does pretty good."

Unbeknownst to Miles and the rest of the nation, Manziel was a player trying to get healthy. Injuries to his knee, his throwing shoulder and now the smashed thumb against Mississippi State had exacted a debilitating toll upon the A&M quarterback. The last malady, the thumb on his throwing hand, was the injury of the most concern to the offensive staff of the Aggies. Manziel was having an impossible time gripping the football and his passes were uncharacteristically inaccurate throughout the two weeks of practice leading to the road trip to Baton Rouge. The uneven throwing sessions and obvious discomfort Manziel was experiencing led head coach Kevin Sumlin to wonder if Manziel should even play against the Tigers. With BCS appearances and a second Heisman on the line, Sumlin knew Manziel, even at a downgraded health, gave his team the best chance to win. Once the decision was made that Manziel would start, all agreed the thumb injury would remain a secret.

If you believe in omens, the weather at kickoff foreshadowed the type of day it would be for Texas A&M. With a biting north wind sending sheets of rain onto the darkening surface of Tiger Stadium, the hindered Manziel led the Aggie offense onto the field to begin the game. The first drive would be a precursor to the frustration the A&M offense experienced over the duration of the game. Penalties, dropped passes, and a wet playing field spoiled the initial charge and plagued the Aggies throughout the first half.

Manziel, hampered by the tender thumb, witnessed several passes sail wide of their intended target. His composure slipping as drive after drive ended without points. Confounding the aggravation was the multiple scoring opportunities the Aggies squandered early in the game. Twice A&M began drives inside the LSU 40 yard line but could only muster a single field goal. A third drive deep into LSU territory ended on downs at the Tigers' three yard line after three straight Manziel incompletions.

While A&M struggled offensively, LSU was forcing the football down the throat of the Aggie defense. Despite an early stand that forced LSU to turn over the ball after failing to convert a fourth down, the A&M defense struggled to stop the Tigers from running for substantial chunks of yardage. LSU scored touchdowns on three of their final four drives of the opening half and with less than two minutes before halftime, the Tigers held a commanding 21-3 lead.

The following A&M drive, a three play push lasting all of 29 seconds, was the day's only highlight for the anemic A&M offense. After a 22 yard completion to LaQuionte Gonzalez, Manziel put the A&M offense in the end zone on the following play, a 51 yard touchdown pass to Derel Walker. Aided by a falling LSU cornerback, an open Walker caught the Manziel pass along the left sideline and sprinted for the end zone. At the LSU two yard line, Walker was met by an LSU defensive back. He stopped and watched as the defender lost his footing and slid out of bounds. Walker eased across the goal line and Manziel had his first ever touchdown against the Tigers. It would also be his last. The halftime score, LSU 21 - A&M 10, was the closest the Aggies would be for the rest of the game.

"We just got punched in the mouth and it wasn't fun," Manziel said moments after LSU finished their 34-10 victory. The loss ended Manziel's perfection on the road, the 40 points or better team scoring streak, and any chance Manziel may have had at a repeat Heisman. The A&M quarterback's line read 16 completions on 41 attempts for a career low 39% completion rate. The ten points and 299 yards of team offense were the lowest totals of the Sumlin-Manziel era.

Kevin Sumlin woke up on the morning of the Missouri game and signed a contract making him a very wealthy man. The new six year deal ended weeks of speculation Sumlin was headed elsewhere and increased the A&M head coach's salary to $5 million per season, making him one of the highest paid coaches in college football. "This is a very sincere, long commitment to an individual who's done a marvelous job in all aspects of the job, from our student athletes, from a competitive standpoint, from the community, from the Aggie family; everybody is extremely excited to have him leading the program," said A&M athletic director Eric Hyman.

Unlike Sumlin, the 2013 Aggies would not have the opportunity to cash in. The loss to LSU narrowed the postseason choices for A&M to a host of second tier December 31st and January 1st bowls, none of which had BCS in the title. This did not mean the game at Missouri meant nothing. It just meant nothing for Texas A&M.

Missouri, on the other hand, was playing for a trip to the SEC championship game. The Tigers entered the SEC with Texas A&M in 2012, and experienced a brutal first year posting a 5-7 record and missing a bowl for the first time in eight seasons. The 2013 turnaround had the Tigers two wins away from a possible berth in the BCS championship game. A remarkable about face earned in part because Missouri became better at running the football and preventing their opponents from doing the same. The rushing offense of the Tigers was ranked 18th in the nation with 238 yards per game, while the Missouri rushing defense held opponents to 113 yards per contest, good for 13th in all of college football.

Missouri's Achilles' heel was their secondary. Unbelievably their pass defense was worse than Texas A&M, as the Tigers allowed 273 yards through the air per game. In contrast, A&M had brought their yardage down to 239 per game. A statistical vulnerability such as the one surrendered by the Missouri defensive backs would have a healthy Manziel foaming at the mouth. Sadly this was not a quarterback whose thumb had improved over the week. Instead, rumblings of Manziel's injury made its way through the media after

160

the LSU game. When asked about the thumb Sumlin said, "If he wasn't healthy enough to play, he wouldn't have played." He wasn't healthy but Manziel would definitely be the quarterback against Missouri.

South Carolina and their fans were watching the game with Missouri and Texas A&M with great interest. A loss by the Tigers, and South Carolina would be headed to the SEC championship game against Auburn, who booked their spot minutes before kickoff, as they beat Alabama on Chris Davis' incredible 109 yard return off a missed field goal. If Manziel was looking for converted A&M fans he would find a host of them in Columbia, South Carolina albeit temporary ones. One young female held up a sign at the Gamecocks home game against non-conference opponent Clemson that read: *Tonight will be the only time I cheer for Johnny Football.*

A&M's first drive didn't see Manziel attempt a pass until the Aggies sixth play. The drive sputtered at midfield and A&M punter Drew Kaser pinned the Tigers at their own 10 yard line. The A&M defense forced a three and out and Manziel took over on the Aggies 35 yard line. Again A&M offensive coordinator Clarence McKinney called for an overwhelming amount of runs. Where the A&M running backs only ran for nine yards on five carries on the first drive, the second attempt to run on the Tigers defense was far more successful. Five rushes on the first six plays moved the football into Missouri territory. Manziel completed three straight flares for 12 yards and watched as Tra Carson took the handoff on the following play 29 yards for the first touchdown of the game. With 6:34 left in the opening quarter A&M led 7-0.

The A&M defense opened the game inspired. After forcing the punt on Missouri's opening drive, the A&M defensive front seven shut down the Tigers running game by swarming the football and making open field tackles, fundamental areas they had struggled with all season. Missouri punted away the football on their first three drives and would not cross the goal line until late in the second quarter as Tigers' starting quarterback James Franklin found Dorial Green-Beckham on a 38 yard touchdown pass.

A&M's drive after Missouri's game tying score began with a Brandon Williams 43 yard run to the Missouri 32 yard line. McKinney then called for three straight passes, the first going to speedy freshman wideout, LaQuvionte Gonzalez, for nine yards. After Manziel was sacked on second down, creating a third and ten, the quarterback took the snap, moved to his left and on the run threw to Derel Walker. The wide receiver, finding a soft spot in the Tigers zone caught the pass on the left sideline, made a move and crossed the goal line. Seventy seconds after Missouri got their first touchdown, A&M had their second. The lead was back to seven in A&M's favor.

On the touchdown pass, as Manziel threw, he was hit from behind by Tigers' left defensive end Michael Sam. The attempted sack wrenched Manziel's left ankle. He hobbled to the sideline and received an extensive exam and fresh tape application. As the half expired Missouri's Andrew Baggett sent a field goal attempt wide to the left and A&M held onto the slim advantage.

With Manziel now hobbled by both hand and foot, the Aggie defense would have to continue their improved play. The Tigers only converted three of nine third downs in the first half, and not counting the Green-Beckham touchdown, had yet to cross the Aggies 29 yard line. Considering the level of opponent, the defense had played their best half of the year.

Missouri opened the second half with their best drive of the game. Running the ball on six of seven plays, the Tigers drove 75 yards in less than three minutes and tied the score at 14. After A&M failed to move the ball on their first drive of the second half, the Tigers scored again as Franklin completed a five yard pass to L'Damian Washington for a touchdown. In eight and a half minutes an A&M lead of seven was now a seven point deficit.

McKinney continued to call runs and bubble screens. The explosive A&M offense was a mere shell of its former self. Slow to the line, slow to snap, the offense failed to get into rhythm. After trading punts the A&M offense was backed up, starting their first drive of the fourth quarter at their own two yard line. McKinney chose this point in the game to loosen the reins on Manziel. The A&M quarterback completed three of his first four passes, moving the football to the

163

A&M 41 yard line. The breathing room allowed the running backs to carry the rest of the burden. Three Trey Williams rushes for 47 yards set up Ben Malena's seven yard plunge across the goal line. With 10:43 left in the fourth quarter, the game was tied at 21.

The A&M defense, settled after allowing the two quick touchdowns, opened Missouri's next drive with a sack on Franklin, the Tigers' quarterback. The seven yard, first down loss by senior linebacker Nate Askew and sophomore defensive tackle Alonzo Williams forced the Tigers into two fruitless pass plays. The resulting punt was met with a matching A&M punt as Manziel could not move the football forward, losing two yards on the three plays.

With 8:08 left in the game, Missouri took over on their own 24 yard line and were stymied once again by A&M's defense. Manziel would have another shot at breaking the tie. Unfortunately for the Aggies, the drive would be nothing short of lackluster. After a nine yard reception by Travis Labhart, Brandon Williams lost three yards on second down and a third down attempt to Mike Evans went incomplete. Kaser booted the punt 50 yards on fourth down to the Missouri 34.

The Tigers ran the ball on the first two downs. Facing a third and one, as the clock fell under four minutes remaining, Missouri called an inside handoff to running back Henry Josey. With the A&M safeties pressed against the line to stuff the expected run, the middle of the football field was susceptible to a big play. As Josey took the handoff, a massive opening

164

emerged along the line of scrimmage. The running back ran 57 yards for the Missouri touchdown. "A big hole opened up and I took it," Josey said. With 3:34 left, Missouri held a 28-21 lead.

This was not the Ole Miss game. Manziel did not look over to Labhart or Evans and smile. He thrashed and screamed and brought the offense from the sideline. The drive opened with a three yard run by Tra Carson. On second and seven, Manziel missed and threw an incomplete pass. McKinney called for a screen to Mike Evans on third down. Evans, all but invisible for 57 minutes of the game, caught the pass, and trying to make something out of nothing, lost six yards. Sumlin decided there was little chance of success on fourth and thirteen, so he kicked the ball away. With two timeouts left, he relied on his defense to stop Missouri.

After a Josey rush on first down for three yards, Franklin faked a handoff on second down and floated a soft pass to the open tight end, senior Eric Waters. The completion went for 16 yards and a first down. Two kneel downs later, the game was over.

As the sold out crowd of 62,000 flooded the field in celebration, a dejected and limping Manziel avoided the surrounding reporters, dressed for the plane ride home, returned to College Station, and did what most former Heisman winners do when they are about to turn 21.

He went to Vegas.

165

12 Duke

He had never lost consecutive games. Nor had he lost a road game as quarterback of Texas A&M. Yet here Johnny Manziel was, physically diminished with his litany of injuries, torn by how the final two games played out.

Good news was Sumlin had given the team two weeks to heal, take their finals, and restore their desire to play football. They wouldn't know where they were playing their bowl game for a week. Conference championships had to be played and their outcomes would affect where the Aggies would finish their season.

Johnny wanted the break. He didn't care where or when they would play next. The game would not be for a BCS championship and that shortcoming wore heavy upon the quarterback. But he was not in the mood to dwell or fall inside himself with his failures. When the itch strikes Manziel, he becomes restless, and eager to gather his friends. One of his biggest passions is travel, so it was little surprise Johnny wanted to put College Station in the rearview over these next several days.

Manziel's destination for relaxation brought murmurs of disappointment from a few individuals, but Las Vegas was the one place Johnny had previously visited where he felt he could disappear. "I was able to walk around the streets (of Vegas) without taking a single picture," Johnny told Andy Staples of Sports Illustrated. "And I was there for a total of seven days over two trips." By all accounts the trip to Sin City, coinciding with Manziel's 21st birthday, was quiet and tame.

Manziel's vacation out west was cut short by the announcement the A&M quarterback was, once again, a finalist for the Heisman Trophy. Chances Manziel would repeat were extinguished a week earlier when Florida's state attorney announced he would not pursue charges against Jameis Winston. The decision had erased any mystery from the Heisman race.

With the trip now a mere formality, Manziel approached the rush of media obligations associated with being a finalist relaxed and open. The man coming to New York City was a year older, a year wiser. At the press conference in Times Square, his largest since SEC Media Days, Manziel was as candid with the gathered press members as he had ever been.

One of the first questions tossed at the native Texan was about his ironic decision to stay relatively quiet during his sophomore season. The reason Manziel's choice to stay silent was so surprising because of the quarterback's previous reaction to Sumlin's team rule that no freshman can speak to the media. Throughout Manziel's Heisman season, he was muzzled, unable to address the hateful remarks pumped at him daily. The quarterback grew frustrated that he was unable to defend himself. Yet, when given the opportunity to address the media throughout his sophomore season, Manziel rarely obliged. It was a contrarian approach the media believed deserved an explanation.

"After the offseason, it was time to shut it down," Manziel said. "I wanted the focus off of me and I wanted it on my teammates. Guys that do so much, and do so much for me, they deserve a lot of the credit. Guys like Jake Matthews and Ben Malena and Mike Evans, they do everything right and they work their tail off every day. My teammates needed to be the focus. Texas A&M Aggies, that's what it needed to be about. It's not the Johnny Manziel Aggies or anything like that. It needed to be about those guys and what I needed to do. I needed to step away."

The focus of the press conference shift to Manziel's future. Several reports issued during Heisman week said Johnny would make a decision on the NFL before A&M's bowl game. Assuring the media and Aggie fans that was false, Manziel said, "No agent talk or anything right now. I'm strictly focused on the bowl game and things will take care of themselves as far as the NFL, more into January, probably."

This did not mean Manziel was modest in his opinion of whether or not he was ready for the professional ranks. "I think me being the way I am, a little bit different, is what makes me special and what makes me a little more dangerous than some other people," Manziel said. "I feel like I continue to get better as a passer to where I need to be to make it at the next level. A lot of work still to do, but I feel like with my instincts and the way I've progressed as a passer, hopefully I'll be ready to make that jump."

Although denying he was looking into the future, Manziel had certainly pondered his legacy. Barring an early injury, the quarterback would break Ryan Tannehill's single season passing yardage record and add to the total of most ever touchdown passes thrown in a year at A&M. If he was about to play his final game as an Aggie, no other player in school history had accumulated more yards (9,534) and touchdowns (88) in a career. The impact Manziel had on the football program at A&M could not be quantified. Proof of this was located 90 miles away in Waco, Texas as Baylor University was experiencing its' greatest football season ever in 2013, two years after Heisman-winning quarterback Robert Griffin III had left to go pro. Benefits provided by Manziel to the health of the Texas A&M football program, would continue many years after he was gone. A fact the quarterback took great pride in.

"The biggest thing for me is driving around the state of Texas now, you see a lot more A&M on the back of cars," Manziel said. "You see a lot more A&M stickers, sweaters, shirts, people really supporting our school. To be a piece of a team the last two years that's helped provide that spark for our fans and Aggies everywhere, to have my input on that is something I'll remember forever."

Manziel placed fifth in the Heisman voting. Winston, Florida State's starting quarterback, finished with 74% of all first place votes, good enough to become the second freshman ever to win college football's most prestigious trophy. A&M's quarterback, the first ever freshman to win the Heisman, was not surprised by the results. "We got a good sense of how things were going to play out. When a guy puts up the numbers that he did and has an undefeated season, there was really no doubt in my mind," Manziel said.

Manziel, awarded the right to vote after his 2012 Heisman win, voted for Winston with his first place vote, Boston College running back Andre Williams second and himself third.

Forthcoming to Winston about what lied ahead, Manziel warned the winner of the dangers associated with the Heisman. "I told him, of all things, don't let this change you. Knowing it was going to happen, I said don't let this change you. Continue to be the guy that you are, don't let anyone change you from that."

Manziel returned to his hotel, repacked his suitcase, and prepared himself for the plane to College Station. His time away from campus was necessary. He needed to clear his mind and restore his body. Feeling whole again now that his thumb, ankle, and shoulder were all regaining strength, Manziel was anxious to get home. He wanted to prove that the last two games were an anomaly; a result created by a ravaged body and exhausted team. Johnny believed all of the uncertainty would go away with a terrific bowl performance. He thought about his bowl opponent, the Duke Blue Devils, on the flight home. They had a New Years' Eve date in Atlanta, home to the Chick-fil-A Bowl.

The quarterback was ready to play.

Manziel returned to College Station and was met by a surprising change in the way the Aggie offense would conduct business against Duke. Offensive coordinator Clarence McKinney had been stripped of play calling duties. Under McKinney, the A&M offense had scored at least 40 points in 13 straight games and totaled over 500 yards in nine straight contests. This was before the disappointing losses to LSU and Missouri. In those two games, the Aggies averaged only 15.5 points and 339 yards. Sumlin believed he was seeing a regression in his offense that needed to change. The bowl game against Duke was far more important to win than the average game. A win against the Blue Devils would keep A&M in the final Top 25 polls and achieve a feat no other Aggie team had ever accomplished – three straight bowl wins. "That's significant," Sumlin said about the win streak. "There's been a lot of football played and a lot of guys who came through (A&M) who can't say they've done that. That can be very, very special to our seniors going out, and that can be

171

something I think that really, really propels us in the offseason."

In McKinney's place, Sumlin elevated 28-year-old quarterbacks coach Jake Spatival to the position. "I just told (Jake) to be confident in what you're doing," Sumlin said. "Be multiple in what you're doing. We'll have some new wrinkles. We're not going to re-invent the wheel in a week and a half, but we'll have a couple new wrinkles. More than anything else, be confident in what you're doing and we'll communicate during the game."

The main thing Sumlin wanted from Spatival was speed. It had been six games since the A&M offense had run 80 plays in a football game. The move to switch offensive coordinator was an attempt to alleviate this problem. Spatival liked to be on the sideline next to the action while McKinney enjoyed the comfort of the press box. The change in location of where the play calls were coming from helped accommodate Sumlin's overall wish to maximize Manziel's plays. "I believe that we might play at a faster pace just due to communication of cutting out the middleman, going from press box to me to Johnny, which is now just a direct communication from me to Johnny," Spatival said. "It's mainly we are just going to try to get a lot of players involved and we are just going to have to find out early in the game who is hot and who is playing well."

The two weeks of practice, in preparation for Duke, returned the spirit and hunger Sumlin saw in the Aggies before the losses to LSU & Missouri. "I like our energy level right now," Sumlin said. "I think guys came back healthy, with a little more bounce in their step. I think we were a little worn down there at the end mentally and physically."

Sumlin's quarterback echoed his coach's sentiments. "I feel really good today. I wish the game was tonight," Manziel said on the eve of the showdown with the Blue Devils. "I'm really tired of having to sit here and continue to practice and continue to wait for the game. I think we are ready to get back on the field. I think we are eager to play. So I was a little banged up – the thumb is feeling extremely well, as well as really everything else, so I feel like I'm healthy and ready to play in the bowl game."

A reinvigorated Manziel, excited Sumlin, and prepared Spatival, gave the 12th Man a jolt of enthusiasm not seen in several weeks. With all the goodwill and confidence surging throughout the Aggie locker room, it was a considerable shock to A&M fans to see Manziel and company line up against Duke and open the Chick-fil-A Bowl with their worst first quarter of the season.

The emotional implosion of Mike Evans ruined any chance Texas A&M had of beginning their matchup as Spatival wanted. The Aggies' first drive, which had advanced to Duke's 23 yard line, was derailed when Evans overreacted to contact in the end zone on a pass thrown by Manziel. Believing strongly that he had been interfered with by the Blue Devils'

173

cornerback, the A&M wideout jumped and screamed into the nearby official's face. The tall Evans brushed his long frame against the official and a flag for unsportsmanlike conduct was thrown. Pushed back near midfield, the drive stalled and a missed goal from Josh Lambo capped the disappointment.

A&M's second drive ended, once again in Duke territory, at the hands of Evans. On a crucial third and ten at the Blue Devils' 27 yard line, the wide receiver ran a crossing route that became the target of Manziel's throw. Evans was able to get both hands on the ball but lost control of the reception when the Duke defensive back slapped the ball away. Lambo was able to connect from 45 yards on his next attempt. The three points would be all A&M could muster in the first quarter.

Evans' antics on the third drive pushed Manziel over the edge. Frustrated by the penalty and dropped pass, Evans decided to take his anger out on a Duke defender by continuing to block the cornerback on an A&M running play far after the whistle had blown. Normally officials would separate the two players but that became impossible once Evans threw the Blue Devil to the ground. A flag was lobbed in the receiver's direction. The unnecessary roughness call pushed A&M back into their own end, seconds after Manziel completed a first down pass to Derel Walker. The drive faltered and Duke was able to block the punt. Moments before that calamity, Manziel rushed off the field, ripped off his helmet, shoved it to the turf, and confronted Evans on the sideline. Johnny demanded

Mike get ahold of himself. Evans did not want to hear the lecture. He pulled away from Manziel and sulked on the bench. Evans' sabotage was compounded by the fact the Aggie defense looked anemic and uninspired. Just over half a minute into the second quarter the Aggie sideline was a mixture of whiplash and disbelief as A&M trailed Duke 21-3.

The Duke Blue Devils came into the Chick-fil-A Bowl celebrating their greatest football season in school history. Sporting a record of 10 wins and 3 losses, Duke found their way to Atlanta by losing 45-7 to Florida State in the ACC Championship. Despite the loss, Duke remained a dangerous team of hard-nosed players, expertly coached by David Cutcliffe. The Blue Devils' specialty of creating turnovers and playing well on special teams allowed the offense to be successful despite posting mediocre numbers. Some argued the Blue Devils were overrated due to several close wins at the end of the season, but through the opening quarter against A&M, Duke had been nothing short of perfect.

Turned away by Duke's defense three straight times, Manziel was forced to watch his counterpart, Blue Devils' quarterback Anthony Boone, eviscerate the A&M defense on his way to three consecutive scoring drives. Boone had only two incompletions over his first three possessions, easily connecting with his receivers for three completions of greater than 25 yards. The quarterback looked relaxed and confident in the pocket, a stark contrast to the flailing Manziel. Each drive that ended in a touchdown for Duke made the Aggie defense look more and more clueless. Several press members wondered aloud why Sumlin felt the offensive coordinator needed replacing but not Mark Snyder, the A&M defensive coordinator. The joke had bite because the Aggies seemed to be ill-prepared to handle whatever Duke sent their way.

Down by eighteen, Manziel and Evans momentarily stopped the bleeding with a short and efficient touchdown drive. The push covered 75 yards in 77 seconds with Evans' 26 yard midfield catch setting up A&M's first touchdown. Manziel connected with slot receiver Travis Labhart on the 23 yard touchdown reception, closing the Duke lead to eleven. There was hope the touchdown would turn the momentum back to A&M. It was a wish that would not be granted.

The next three drives would end in touchdowns. Boone threw his second touchdown of the day, a 59 yard bomb to Jamison Crowder. Manziel answered with his second scoring throw to Labhart. The touchdown flurry concluded with Duke running back Josh Snead's second touchdown run, making the score 35-17 in favor of the Blue Devils. Duke had crossed the goal line on all five of their first half possessions.

With less than three minutes before halftime, the Blue Devils lined up to kick the ball back to A&M. Cutcliffe made the call for an onside kick. The Aggies' kick return unit looked as hopeless as the

176

defense. Duke easily recovered the ball at the 50 yard line and A&M was on the door of extinction.

But then something strange happened. Although the call was made to risk the onside kick, Duke's offense became passive and aloof. Four straight running plays were called by Cutcliffe and minutes drained from the clock. Killer instinct had given way to contentment. The Blue Devils did not appear to be interested in adding another touchdown. Duke settled for a field goal as time expired and the two teams headed to their locker rooms staring at a scoreboard that read Duke 38, Texas A&M 17.

In thirty minutes of football the A&M defense had surrendered 365 yards, 38 points and a staggering 10.1 yards per play. The halftime deficit of 21 points had never been overcome by an A&M team. Walking around the locker room, senior running back Ben Malena saw nothing but grim faces. He stood in front of his teammates, at the halftime of his last college football game, and offered a simple challenge. "Do you want to be embarrassed on national television?" Sumlin was next. His speech urged the team to not giving up on one another. It will take each one of you giving everything you have, the coach pleaded. The team surrounded Sumlin, put their hands in the middle and broke for their last half of the 2013 season. The message from Malena and Sumlin was clear, to defeat Duke, the Aggies would have to be flawless.

The A&M defense, absent for the entire first half, showed life on Duke's opening drive of the third quarter. After the Aggies began the half with a kickoff to Duke, the A&M front seven stonewalled the Blue Devils' running back, Juwan Thompson, on a fourth and one. Euphoria erupted from the Aggie sideline as A&M's offense was given its' first shot at reducing Duke's enormous lead.

Manziel was unreal on A&M's initial drive of the second half. A dizzying mixture of keepers, screen passes, and tackles broken up by the agile A&M quarterback moved the ball inside Duke's 20 yard line. On second and seven, Manziel dropped back to pass, and what happened next was celebrated as one of the top plays of 2013.

Manziel completed his drop step and surveyed the field. All his receivers were covered. Without a throwing option, the quarterback tried to extend the play. Sensing a push from the right defensive end, Manziel moved a few steps forward. Looking upfield, Johnny did not see the Duke linebacker racing toward him from the left. The defender lunged head first at Manziel. Spotting the blind side rusher a heartbeat before being sacked, the quarterback jumped straight into the air. The linebacker dove into Manziel's airborne legs and the contact forced the quarterback to twist awkwardly. The hit was so effective that the players momentarily seemed to freeze. But Manziel inexplicably did not fall to the turf. Instead he bounced off the back of an Aggie lineman and landed upright on his size 15 feet. Manziel popped out of the chaos, rolled to his left, and floated a pass to a stunned Labhart. The receiver caught the throw and coasted into the end zone.

The quarterback ran to the sideline, climbed upon an equipment box in front of the A&M section of fans, and demanded more noise. He removed his helmet, grabbed a towel and sat, in time to watch Thompson run for 41 yards on Duke's first play, advancing the ball to A&M's 34 yard line. He cursed and buried his head in the towel. The frustration could no longer stay within. Manziel began to cry in frustration. The thought that another game would be wasted by an ineffective defense was far too much to once again swallow.

But the defense held. Duke's field goal attempt was shanked to the left and Manziel returned to the field with a chance to cut Duke's lead to seven. Aided by Spatival, the quarterback took advantage of the offense coordinator's new wrinkles and continued to establish a rhythm. Slinging the ball to the sidelines, Manziel made his best throw of the drive on a play action rollout, finding rarely used tight end Cameron Clear for 30 yards. Tra Carson caught a Manziel lateral, and aided by an unseen Labhart hold, raced up the left sideline for a 21 yard touchdown. The 12th Man was on fire as the Aggies had reversed Duke's first half momentum and made the score 38-31.

Duke's third drive of the quarter was denied by another A&M stand. Moving the ball easily inside the Aggies five yard line, the Blue Devils failed to cross the goal line, settling for three points and a 41-31 lead, as the fourth quarter began.

Manziel was a double edged blade in A&M's opening drive of the final quarter. Slashing at Duke with both arm and legs, the quarterback completed all three passes, including a gorgeous back shoulder throw along the right sideline to Evans, advancing the ball to Duke's three yard line. From there, Manziel took the shotgun snap, faked a handoff to Malena and bootlegged out to the left flat. Seeing an open path to the end zone, Manziel sped to the left pylon and entered the end zone just before he was hit by a Duke defender. The score cut Duke's lead to three.

The quarterback did not rest as the extra point was tried. He found members of the defense, and demanded they continue to fight. "I want it back!" Manziel said.

A&M's defense almost granted Manziel's wish. Forcing five third downs on the following drive, the Aggies couldn't seem to deliver the knockout blow to get off the field. Instead Duke's quarterback made play after play, 14 in fact, on a drive lasting over six minutes, capped by Boone's touchdown pass to David Reeves. The lead was back to ten.

The beauty, and perhaps curse, of the A&M offense was their ability to score fast. With less than seven minutes left in the game and facing a two possession deficit, Manziel answered Boone's long drive in 62 seconds. The touchdown came on a 44 yard rainbow throw from Manziel to wideout Derel Walker. The receiver caught the ball and fell into the end zone for Manziel's fourth touchdown pass of the game. Duke's lead was once again slim at 48-45.

After Thompson's long run, the one that pushed Manziel to the verge of emotional collapse, the A&M defense had been stingy with Duke's running backs. Cutcliffe, knowing that Duke would need more than a field goal, mixed his calls on the Blue Devils' drive that began with under six minutes remaining in the game. Two Snead rushes for ten yards sandwiched a 15 yard completion from Boone. At midfield, Duke seemed to be in a groove, looking at a manageable second down and five to go.

Boone received the shotgun exchange and focused in on receiver Johnell Barnes on a short pass. Reading the play was A&M cornerback Toney Hurd Jr. As Boone raised the ball to throw, Hurd made a break toward Barnes. Hurd beat the throw, stepped in front of the receiver, picked off Boone's pass, and ran the other way for a potential go ahead touchdown.

The Aggie cornerback had only one Blue Devil to beat, the man who made the throw, Boone. Sprinting down the left sideline, Hurd met Boone at the ten yard line. The quarterback dove for Hurd's legs and missed. The senior crossed the goal line and A&M had their first lead of the game, 52-48. The A&M sideline and the 12th Man exploded in joyous disbelief.

Three and a half minutes remained on the clock when Boone brought Duke's offense on the field for their final drive of the game. Pushed by the rejuvenated A&M defense to a third down and seven, Boone was resilient with a deep ball to Crowder, good

181

for 23 yards. On the next series, the Duke offense was forced into a fourth and four. Again the Duke quarterback answered the challenge with a five yard completion to Brandon Braxton.

Duke was at the Aggie 38 yard line. A first down pass to Crowder was broken up in the end zone. The clock was nearing 90 seconds. Snyder decided on second down to send A&M cornerback Deshazor Everett on a blitz.

The gamble paid off.

Boone dropped back in the pocket and didn't see Everett until it was too late. The Aggie defensive back grabbed Duke's quarterback high upon the jersey and attempted to wrench him to the ground. Inexplicably Boone tried to make a play. He flicked the ball away, hoping to stop the clock with an incompletion. Instead the pass wobbled and fell gently into the waiting hands of A&M linebacker Nate Askew. Returning the interception just three yards, Askew was mobbed by his teammates as he fell to the turf.

In a game that saw the A&M defense give up 48 points, 661 total yards and never once forced their opponent to punt, the beleaguered group of young men made two improbable plays that clinched the victory for A&M.

As Manziel kneeled down for the third time and watched the last second fall from the clock, a strange mix of confetti and foam cows with parachutes attached (a marketing ploy from Chick-fil-A) fell from the rafters of the Georgia Dome. The quarterback made his way through a congratulating crowd, found his head coach and hugged him.

The media surrounded Manziel.

"I was in a zone I haven't been in before," the quarterback said. "Ever. I just wanted this game."

The unlikely path of Johnny Manziel's sophomore season ended with one final speech. Moments after receiving the game's most valuable offensive player award, Manziel, still in pads, stood in front of the fans that remained in the Georgia Dome and thanked them for their unending support. Before, during, and after his words, the traveling 12th Man begged the quarterback to stay with chants of "one more year." Beaming, Johnny told the crowd how proud he was to be an Aggie.

Throwing for 382 yards, running for another 73, and responsible for five touchdowns, Manziel's second half performance was the greatest reason the 2013 Aggies were able to pull off the biggest comeback in Texas A&M history. "We got beat by a great football player," said Duke head coach David Cutcliffe. "He truly is. He showed today. He may have played as well today as he's played all season."

Manziel was asked repeatedly during postgame interviews if the win made it easier to leave for the NFL. He refused to answer the question, instead showering praise upon the teammates he played with all season. "I love them more than anything on the face of the earth," Manziel told ESPN's Samantha Ponder.

The feeling was mutual. Weeks later Mike Evans was asked about playing with Manziel. "It was a great experience playing with one of my best friends," Evans said. "He's a great playmaker. Being a part of his success, I love him to death. He throws a great ball and throws it away from the defender where I can get it. Great teammate. I'd go to war with him anytime."

Evans was the first eligible Aggie to declare for the NFL draft. Citing his family and the potential windfall of a lucrative contract as the reason, the wide receiver decided to forgo his final two seasons. The announcement made all eyes turn to Manziel. He was in no hurry. Relishing the accolades that poured in after his bowl performance, the quarterback enjoyed a trip to Los Angeles. Making an appearance at the BCS Championship game, Manziel remained quiet about his future plans.

In the meantime, draft experts were bumping Johnny to the top of their boards. Slotted in the top five in most of the latest mock drafts, College Station became resigned to the notion their quarterback might not be an Aggie much longer. Perhaps it was impossible to continue to believe he would stay at the one place where his impulsiveness and blind ambition was rewarded with an unending loyalty that chased away his doubt. They knew he would always need the respect of those who hated him. Forever, he would seek new converts to the church of Johnny Football.

Manziel did not inform the world of his decision with a glossy and bombastic public spectacle. Rather he did so quietly, with a simple press release. He wanted to thank those fans that stood all year and loved him. He wanted them to know how grateful he was for their allegiance. To those individuals, to the 12th Man, Johnny Manziel had one final thing to say.

To All My Friends in Aggieland,

After long discussions with my family, friends, teammates, and coaches, I have decided to make myself available for the 2014 NFL Draft. The decision was not an easy one. Anyone who has ever watched a football game at Kyle Field knows that leaving that atmosphere, those Saturdays with excitement, color, and noise, will be hard for me. I cannot begin to tell you what the support of the school, my teammates, Coach Sumlin, Chancellor Sharp and the fans has meant to me over the last two years. The Heisman Trophy belongs as much to you as it does to me. My teammates and I never doubted the value or the deep and real spirit of The 12th Man. It is not a myth. Anyone who has ever played football for Texas A&M knows that passion is real.

I promise you I will always be an Aggie. I will always try to make you as proud of me in the NFL as I did at Texas A&M. While there are many wonderful memories I will take with me – big wins, surprising upsets, and Bowl victories – I most cherish standing arm in arm with my teammates during the postgame, singing the alma mater, or jumping into the stands to feel the real Aggie spirit. I regret we weren't able to bring home a National Championship to College Station, but I assure you a championship is going to come soon with Coach Sumlin and these talented players. And when it does, you can bet I will be with you to cheer and celebrate. I'll probably be the loudest one there.

Thank you for making my college years very special. The faces, the friends, the fans, and the experience will forever be an important part of my life. Gig 'em Aggies! I'll always love you guys.

> *Sincerely,*
> *Johnny Manziel*
> *January 8, 2014*

Manziel's 2013 Stats

2013 Game Log		Passing		Rushing	
Week	OPP	YDS	TD	YDS	TD
1	Rice	94	3	19	0
2	SHSU	426	3	36	1
3	Alabama	464	5	98	0
4	SMU	244	1	102	2
5	@Arkansas	261	2	59	0
6	@Ole Miss	346	0	124	2
7	Auburn	454	4	48	1
8	Vanderbilt	305	4	11	0
9	UTEP	273	4	67	2
10	Miss. State	446	5	47	0
11	@LSU	224	1	54	0
12	@Missouri	195	1	21	0
Bowl	Duke	382	4	73	1
	Season Totals	4114	37	759	9

Sources

My primary fountain for information regarding Johnny Manziel's sophomore season came from College Station's newpaper the *Eagle*. I cannot imagine there is a group of reporters who do a better job of covering their local college football program than those working for the *Eagle*. I have tried to credit reporters who receive direct quotes, any mistakes are unintentional. Visit AggieSports.com and MyAggieNation.com for archived stories from Manziel's two seasons at A&M.

Other articles of great interest and use were:

Wright Thompson's profile of Manziel titled "The Trouble with Johnny" in August 19th, 2103 issue of *ESPN The Magazine,* "Johnny on the Spot" by Andy Staples in the August 5th, 2013 issue of *Sports Illustrated*, and the Bloomberg.com article titled "Manziel's Heisman Brought Texas A&M About $20,000, School Says," by Curtis Eichelberger from November 1st, 2013. Also quotes were pulled from post-game reports by the Associated Press.

Again any failure to properly credit an article and its' author is unintentional and will be corrected on future editions.

Author's Note

Once I read a quote from an author explaining that each movie made is a miracle. I believe that creating a book from scratch is no different. It takes a village of caring, devoted individuals to make the dream come true. To the following people I offer my gratitude, and my love, for their support in the process of writing Johnny Sophomore.

My sincere thanks go to: Mom, Dad, Ainsley, Chloe, Granny, Mam-Maw, Chris, Tish, Kathi, Don, Shelly, JR, Kristy, Alan, Donny, Cade, Lyn, Michelle, Missy, Paul, Chris, Winston, Dr. Robert, Ken, Jan, Chad, Tom, Shawn, Ryan, Tracy, Saundra, Joe, Andrea, Nolan, Stales, Kyle, Brent, Melanie, Nikki, Brandi, Liz, Phyllis, Mike, Kevin, Collin, Claire, Anna, and Aiden Spieth.

Made in the USA
San Bernardino, CA
24 October 2018